AN UNPLANNED MERRIMENT

UNFOLDING MYSTERIES OF AN UNFORGETTABLE JOURNEY

DHEERAJ KUMAR

This book is dedicated to my sweet parents.

Father and Mother

I love you.

and to all my Brothers, Sisters,

And my dear Love Kevin Kumar.

Contents

Introduction

There is a sense of adventure in which this text invoked a cliche, not only in the writer but also in the readers, because the book sums up, what most everyone could pointedly relate with. It is rare for a literary piece to charge and evoke so much emotion in the readers such that they feel like they themselves are part of the characters because they could feel their own personality in one character or the other. There is far more to this work than meets the eye; the further it is explored, the more it offers. The elements of the story can well deflect and reflect the attention from the modernity that it exposes.

It may be helpful to quite approach this story from different perspectives and angles. The book employs so many artistic elements and at the same time embeds them. From the elements of characterization to setting and really wide attention on the plot and the plot twist of the story.

The story avails us the opportunity to look into a certain part of the lives of each character and at the same time. figure out what they all have in common, the unifying terminology that brings them all together. The adventures of three friends who just graduated and at the same time one of them is about to marry.

Dheeraj Kumar doubles as the central character and at the same time the narrator of the story. The story literally revolves around him. His journey through the university and now he is a graduate and is ready to get married. His being the narrator of the story gives readers an insight into the in-depth message of the book itself. Using the first-person narrator and pronounced. Dheeraj Kumar is able to give his own account of all that transpired during the course of their journey. It also intimates readers with the kind of life Kumar leads. His being the mouthpiece is not any form of the mistake but an artistic means of relaying the message and intent of the characters to the audiences. His character throws more light on other characters in such a way that we see these characters, not as typical characters but as figures which depict a part of our society.

Through characterization, we could see other characters like Ali and Sidra, who were both key role players in the plot of this story. Ali could be described to be the support to the lead character. His character explains kore about the central character and also foreshadows some of his traits as narrator and the character taking the lead role. His character serves as a stand-in for the central character, somewhat what we can call a keeper or guardian angel. They both have some similarities which go a long way in describing who they are and their peculiarities in day-to-day life.

There are quite a few flat characters who also contribute to the development of the plot of the story. To a great extent, the characters create some figures that are relevant in modern-day society. This depicts the modernist tendency of the text.

The settings are of different Geographical locations each showing different coordinates. Islamabad, Karachi, Quetta, Thar, etc all depict nothing but adventures. adventures on its own is quite a major theme of the work and the messages intended to pass across are solidified by the use of language and the extreme sophistication of style and literary terms.

The use of language also contributes to how the story is shaped into the contemporary Pakistan setting and reality. The simple language employed makes it easy for the readers to intimate themselves with the happenings in the book itself and also gives them an open chance to place characters into day-to-day life and also fit them into characteristics that portray their full potential.

It may be helpful to approach these conclusions by making it a way of simplicity. With the wonderful narrative energy, we can virtually see the carrier of the message itself, owing to the direct theme of the story.

Conversations by characters in the story are embedded with adventurous registers that depict the way the characters are and the way they relate with themselves.

The text creates an impressive line to the depth and range of the main character's thoughts covering many issues that resonate around the central character. His life to religion, academics, friendship, and other aspects of individual life. The text in a way could be said to be the reflection of the day-to-day activities as seen in the text itself. Severally, figurative text not only superficially espouses readers to the things that are within their immediate environment but also points out the point at which the societal confluence is created.

CHAPTER ONE

GOODBYE ISLAMABAD

A good morning to wake up to the brightness of my student-sized room in the heart of Islamabad, but not complete without the buzzing of the commercial heartbeat of this huge city. I have had to live up to this for the past five years of my life, although the whole experience is worth it. The ecstasy I woke up with could not be matched with any other thing, I believe I have never felt this way special. Today I am rounding up my degree at Islamabad University.

"What a rollercoaster of knowledge and experience" I smiled to myself on my bed as reminisced on how it all started five years. The young man from a little town with a bag full of dreams whose passion and hunger for success drove me to the heartbeat of Pakistan, where I actually what to bring to realization all my daydreams and goals.

The goal of coming to the city had never for once changed but the thirst keeps being on the rise. Today I'll be writing my final exams and that will be all on why I am here.

"I have taken it upon myself, to make you proud and be fulfilled," I told my mother when everything was set for me to leave Tharparkar, my hometown.

The dream on this day has grown bigger and different from the little daydream in my hometown. Now I am planning to get married to the love of my life just after rounding off my program here. My Dear Tara, I whom I took so much delight in. I had known her for quite some time now but with the intervention of my mother, I could win her heart to me. I love her so much. Five years away in the land where I knew no one, but now it looks like I am flowing in a pool of friends, good ones at that.

From my first day in Islamabad, God had blessed me with good people. Ali had been my very good and great friend, right from when we met at the train station.

"I can see you have so much luggage, I don't mind helping you with some" the gentle voice had spoken behind me with a little touch on my shoulder. I turned by in surprise at the stranger's utterance and to also ascertain who that was. A young man with a smiling face, whose smile beams so well and could ignite a smile from the other person, was putting on a white sparkling shirt which in all ways speaks an aura of peace and it evokes a kind of personality that is beyond the norm. He was putting on a face cap and black sunglasses. All these are what complements his stand like a gentleman and someone one would always look forward to talking to. I was greeted with a very big smile, "I am Ali Haider" he had immediately retorted not letting me utter a word but immediately collecting a bag from me.

"Dheeraj, Dheeraj Kumar" that's all I can utter, in shock disbelief.

Ali's smile is accompanied by the closure on his white teeth and his look is kind of saintly which puts my mind at rest about who he is.

The number of times Ali himself had given himself to the people was quite more than the ones he has ever had for himself in his lifetime, sacrificing lots and putting himself in the line for the people whom he loved. He shows love immensely to the ones he loves and would always go all out for the ones he loves.

This act of kindness from who turned out to be my best friend in Islamabad birthed a smooth and healthy relationship between us, five years and still strong. Although not with differences but we have come to the realization of our interpersonal differences and we both are of the opinion that tolerance is key. Just like the popular saying in Tharparkar where I'm from that "with tolerance, you can risk ten demons for one angel" this just perfectly describes what's in existence between us two. Ali my quite reserved, clever, and smart friend would go all the way to make things easy for his loved ones, this he had shown me so many times. The figure that I saw on this day won my soul, body, and spirit. Ali was so pure in spirit and soul.

In my second year in Islamabad, Ali had assisted me in putting together a whole lot of things as regards finances. I had little or no financial support or assistance as of then, but he had helped me get back on my feet through supports and aids which he provided for me at this point.

Ali had once started selling car spare parts online at that period.

I began to wonder how he would be able to combine both academics and the business aspect but to my utmost surprise, he excelled at both, but he had kept the business from his parents and family members.

Ali was so kind to me that he would give me money out of his business. There was a time I challenged him concerning how he gives me money out of the ones meant for his business.

"Not worry brother, everything will just be as perfect as alright" he had assured me once when I was lost in the thoughts of how I was going to make money. He introduced me to one or two of his friends who also helped me secure a little job which made me financially buoyant which even the result extended to my family. He had such a large heart, he nearly does not really care about money, he placed relationships above all that.

"What matters most is what we share amongst ourselves" he would say.

Ali's mother, even hearing about my marriage plan, sent some special gifts to my mother. It is a specially made dress which she specifically handpicked for her as a present for her son's wedding. One can easily trace Ali's cheerfulness to his parents because it runs so well in their blood.

Ali and I had both been through quite a lot of things together. A good example was a time we both had a little accident. We had to ho deliver a Mehran car cover to Ali's customer in Saddar, Rawalpindi. We both were on the bike. Ali is the one who knows how to drive the bike, why I do not move close to it. On this faithful day, Ali and I were having a conversation on the bike. The man who was right behind us came all of a sudden to hit us from behind. The shock of this displaced us off the bike. Ali fell on the road, and he suffered a painful bruise on his shoulder. I was well and good if not for the little injury on me.

Ali and I had to keep this to ourselves and away from Ali's family because he would not want to have any issue with them as regards this.

Mother had felt this personally and even enjoyed my friendship with Ali. She had always loved my choice of friends, from childhood till the present day.

Something about me is my ability to discern if my intentions are pure and genuine. To figure this out isn't always hard for me as I could read who you are, hence why catching up with Ali was quite easy. He was also studying in the same University as me and we mostly had time to hang out and also mingle with friends.

Islamabad is a city to be in, right from beautiful sights to a peaceful environment although the city is always busy due to the influx of several commercial activities which serves as the engine that has been running the city. You definitely would want to explore the city which prompted Ali and me to take a tour of the city.

The misty clouds and dew seemed to be the best atmospheric conditions to climb the mighty Margalla hill. One of the greatest experiences so far in the whole city in a space of five years. I had fun alongside my jolly friend Ali.

"It is really a great sight to see," Hamza, one of Ali's classmates had told us about the hill which had been in existence long centuries ago.

"I heard so much about the huge hill, would love to be there one day" Ali added to what Hamza had said.

"Maybe we go there on our next picnic," I suggested to Ali, making him know we can as well go there on our next picnic. One of the things that have become habitual for Ali and me is our monthly picnics, which served as our means of refreshing and getting away from all University. They were fun and as usual; experiences we would want to have and at the same time recreate. We had time to discuss and also intimate ourselves on our plans and resonate on things to do.

We made arrangements for our next picnic, and it was nothing short of fun and excitement.

"This is beyond majestic and great" I exclaimed at the sight of one of the biggest paths on the hill.

"This has always been people's comment" the seemingly unsurprised tour guard replied. Ali was not interested in our talks because it would distract him, but he was rather focused on enjoying the serenity of the environment and at the same time, savoring the beauty of the environment. The Daman E Koh (Hilltop) was so a beautiful sight to behold, seeing the beauty of the city from a bird's eye view. We had several other moments together which builds up the strength of our friendship.

He has vouched for his own support for my wedding, and he is ready to assist in any way. That is just who he is.

"In case there is any way I can come in, do not hesitate to let me know" he had opined knowing fully well the implications. All I could do at the moment was to show some appreciation.

"What do you plan for after examination?" I asked him at one of our evening eat-outs at a local restaurant G10 Markaz.

He stylishly lifted his head which was earlier fixed towards the food, with his mouth slightly open.

"I will figure it out just when I am done with the examination, brother let us enjoy the moment" he replied in his funny manner. I looked at him in admiration of our friendship. Been quite a smooth journey.

"Mom just wrote to me that everything is going well as planned and the marriage rites will take place just after my final examination," I told Ali about what's on the ground at the moment.

"Oh then, that's nice a plan and you know, I will always be down for the brother". He assured me again in his usual self.

Mom and the family back at home have been making different plans as regards the marriage rite, all making different plans for the coming marriage between their son who had gone to the city to study and now, he is not only coming back home as a graduate but at the same time to get married. The dreams coming quite true.

"I am thinking we could go together after the examination" Ali had to suggest suggested with an indifferent look in his. I knew right away that he was super excited. The fact that he would be going with me right from the conclusion of the examination gave him the impression that he would be able to do lots alongside, which include explore, adventures and also the views.

"That is definitely what I have been waiting for, come along let's go see some sights brother" I commended him with excitement in my voice and the glow on my face.

The journey of a thousand miles as they say. I jerked back into reality, noting that I have to brace my mind as it is a quite big day ahead of me. Just a step to finish the line and a step into another life. My friend on the other hand is on his own verge, trying to also put things together as we approach the end of our studies. It's really a good moment.

I set myself ready for the big day ahead, to sum everything up with success.

I made my way through the teeming crowd of students in the corridor that leads to the hall. Chatters of students who are excited could be heard, even from the farthest end of the corridor. With a composure that could be second to none, I matched into the hall to get it done and dusted with. Within a couple of hours, I was done, and a big optimistic smile took over my face. With joy radiating all over, one could tell how happy I am.

I immediately set out for where Ali and I had planned to meet up just after our papers. Grinning right some feet before me is my friend whose aura of joy and happiness triples mine.

"Maybe you need to walk faster" he beckons at me, seeing how my pace was as I also beam in happiness.

"It is a time worthy of it here, five years filled with wonderful experiences," I said as we moved closer to each other.

One of the days that flashed through my mind at the moment is one of those days when I was a member of a non-governmental organization. That was in my second year of study. At this NGO in which I was a volunteer member, I had the opportunity to meet with several people, people with the same thoughts and opinions. Amongst some of the people I met was a beautiful lady named Alize. She was a bright mind, whom most times we deliberate on theories that would be beneficial to the human race and tribe. We both enjoyed working together as we had the chance to work on a freelance writing project. Her wit and wisdom are as far wide as the horizon. I cherish her reasoning and point of thought. After some time, Alize and I both started a blog where we showcased our writings, and truth be told, our articles and writing went so really far and wide as we began to have an influx of readers and clicks on the blog day in day out.

Alize once informed me about meeting her friend, whom she knows I would be interested in meeting.

"I would love to introduce my close friend to you. She is a fan of your blogging work," she said. As she hints me about this friend whom she would want me to meet.

"I would be excited and eager to meet her," I said in surprise at who the fan is.

Well, it is time for me to meet with Sidra. My friend had made arrangements for us to meet at a coffee shop, TYTO COFFEE SHOP. The shop was around the Park premises availing is the opportunity and luxury of time to discuss and both share ideas.

I got to see the beautiful figure, Sidra whose beauty swept me quite off my feet. Her cool, calm, and reserved first impression thrilled a lot within me.

"I believe you have a cool personality which draws one towards you," I remarked, as I marveled at her modesty on meeting with her

"Thank you so much" she showed her appreciation in the modest of all forms ever. One can tell she's a lady of charisma, from the way she talks to her composure. This prompted me to talk to her and I was not disappointed with what was before me. Having a fact and quick reality check on here makes me realize how well we hold ourselves together and how most people end up being in a circle. My circle of friends is what I will always be boastful of. Owing to the fact that we all look inwardly in choosing one another.

In the twinkle of an eye, we got really engulfed in our little talks, there I got to know a few things about her. She currently studies physiotherapy at Shifa college, but she has quite an interest in politics and economics. I had earlier wondered why she was so fervent and fastidious when we talked about the condition. The country's economic and political status. She had backed every bit of her points up with references from the historical and political background and so well-grounded interest in grass-root politics.

"The politics at the grass-roots need so much reform. There should be no matter how little it is some sensitization for the people at the rural level towards cheering them and preparing them for governance and also the need for them to be peaceful and law-abiding" She posed her own opinion to me which I feel is one to always key into as she gave an insight into one of the major issues that tackles our communication. The level at which sensitization is needed is high and recommendable.

I got swept away by her personality and the way she carries herself.

"No gainsaying, she has a very pure spirit and soul," I thought to myself, because who would not want to be close with such an excellent personality?

We since then kept in contact all because we enjoy each other's company. Although we do not get to see each other, we still find time around the clock to meet up.

I met with Ali the following day and explained the mouth-watering experience I had the previous day with Sidra

"I met with a female chap yesterday, Alize introduced me to her" I had said to Ali who was partially listening to me and at the same time feeding his eyes with the shenanigans going on outside the window.

"Hmm" he heaves and continued "tell me more"

"She is Alize's friend. I got introduced to her because she likes my blogs and I appreciate her also. She is brilliant and brainy. Kind of women our society needs

I also introduced Sidra to my friend Ali, which they both got along with, and I never for once regret introducing them to each other.

We all would meet once a week just to have good talks and discuss our plans for studies and life in totality.

Eventually, Sidra receives a job offer from AKU and is going to move away from Islamabad. She will soon begin her internship at AKU.

I still remember that day when she called to let me know the news.

"Dheeraj Bro, I have good and bad news for you guys. Why don't we three watch the Bumblebee Movie together?" Sidra said to me on the phone.

"Bad news! Is everything OK?" I replied and simultaneously wondered what the bad news could possibly be.

"No, don't worry, just tell Ali about today's plan and meet me at Saddar Cinema at 5 PM, where we'll watch a Bumblebee movie and I'll tell you all the details".

I call Ali and tell him about the movie plan.

Well, it was time for us to watch a movie and know about the bad and good news.

After watching the movie, we went to the closest cafe and ordered some burgers and soft drinks.

"I have received an internship offer for one year at AKU. It has always been my dream to work at Pakistan's most prestigious hospital, so now I am beyond thrilled!" Sidra said.

"OMG, and congratulations sis" I wished.

"Wow, what great news! We are very happy, and this is a piece of good news, isn't it?" Ali exclaimed happily.

"Yes, yes." She responded whilst sipping a cold drink.

"And, how about the bad news?" I asked.

This coming Monday is the first day of work, so I will depart Islamabad on Saturday." She informed.

All the good memories of Islamabad flood into my head as Ali and I rummage over our next plan of action which was to devise our travel plans out of the city.

The plans for the wedding are so ongoing, we at least have to go on a shopping spree also, in order to get the necessities for all the marriage rites to be performed and even our own personal effects. Shopping for them before the wedding will ease a lot.

Ali on the other hand had me following my suggestion with some intermittent looks to affirm that he is with me on it, he literally picked it up from where I stopped, and he gave a brilliant suggestion.

"I'd suggest we go to Karachi for the shopping, we'll have the luxury of choices and definitely would hop on the best, trust me," he said and continues immediately "and from there we might see some sights before heading home to have a really nice time" he concluded looking into my eyes as if the words were boldly written in my eyes and he's only trying to read the legible words.

I must say that idea is brilliant. We both agree on making preparing for Karachi and in a couple of days, we would be en route to Karachi, straight out of Islamabad after five years of studies. Going home as a bachelor's degree holder and at the same time a husband-to-be.

We plan to stay some days in Karachi, shop and have a little fun then proceed to another city which we have not even found out which. But definitely, we are calling it goodbye to the city of Islamabad.

The D-Day is here, and streams of emotions started flowing in. I looked out of the train's window just to reminisce about the beautiful moments we have had for years in Islamabad.

It has really been a roller coaster ride.

Thank you, Islamabad

CHAPTER TWO

WEDDING RING

The launching into a new life just began, the life outside Islamabad. Today, we're bidding our five years of sojourn a really big goodbye.

The fast-moving train leaves a track in my heart which marks an unforgettable memory in my head. The hot afternoon reminds me solely of my very first trip to Islamabad to secure my place in the entrance examination which turned out so well. Being the first of such a long journey I was so terrified that I watched how the trees moved past the fast-moving train, just by like a baby. My heart skipped out of fear because I've never traveled this long.

Ali who is far deep into the comic book he's reading never really paid attention to the pace at which the train is moving. He got so engrossed in what he's reading that I had to tap him back to life.

"The fast-moving train reminds me of lots of my childhood memory and even some adulthood, "I said, to spark up a conversation.

"Oh yeah, but I never paid attention to the speed, I am only enjoying the cruise this comic book is giving," he says as he tries to show me what he has been up to.

"Yeah, some cool vibes" I added to what he said as I also took a glance at the cool vibes my friend is talking about. The comic book at a glance talk about trust and how a community betrayed another over and over again just because of a little piece of jewel. Ali is quite a fund of reading comic books "They are educative and at the same time entertaining" he'd say, to support his notion of reading comics.

He opted to give me one of his comic books which he told me he cherished so much.

"I'd say you should read this, quite educative a book," he said to me as he offered me the book titled "Solitude". I found this boring and weird, just like watching cartoons. I flip through the pages of the book and found a few lessons to learn, although the fact remains that the book is quite boring but still educative.

A part of the book that talks about honesty and loyalty got a huge part of me all because I am really big on that. I cherish honesty and loyalty over anything. Even my friends know me so well that I am huge on that and they know how far I can go on these notions. Now I have a point of interest in the comic text which definitely defines and shapes how well I view the content of the book but still could not fathom how Ali had developed so much interest in the book. Well here comes to play the place of interpersonal differences. Just like one of my aversion, Ali loves cartoon animation. These were what made up his childhood, and how he was raised. From a middle-class family of four with three girls, he had no choice but to do most "Girl things".

"It's quite funny how I blended with the girls" he once said in a discussion about his background.

Part of why I am quite excited about his decision on going with me to Karachi, his sense of fashion and design is at the same time top-notch. He has a very high taste for if not everything, design. In particular, he seems to find it quite easy, and he finds his way around it so easily.

We're just halfway into the journey when Ali called my attention to our prior shopping list. He definitely came to my rescue on this by giving a sound opinion on the kind of designs we would be needing for my traditional wedding. He knows I'm open to opinions and suggestions so far it is going to be beneficial to all the parties involved.

"There is a new trend in marriage clothing. It is called Sherwani. We would check it out when we get to Karachi" he had rounded off. I did not probe him further know it because I know we would see it in Karachi once we start shopping and if I am fascinated by it, we are going for it".

The loud buzz of the Trains horn woke virtually everyone up. With my eyes slightly opened, I could see people at the terminal going about their different businesses. The traders on one hand are fully focused on their wares beckoning people to come to patronize them. Then the travelers, on the other hand, some scampering around to get their luggage together and at the same time people who help passengers with their loads just for a little sun of money.

The thought of the clearance process clouded my mind so much that I almost forgot that my friend, my brother is also with me on the journey. He had to call on me to make me know, I was lost in thoughts. How funny. We got to the clearance point and it did not even take long before we got cleared.

"Let the shopping spree begin," Ali said to me patting my back as we walked down the large walkway that leads to the parking lot where we'd journey to our destination.

I have in me this sense of fulfillment as the journey into progress and it all seemed like we're in a new world. Firstly, I feel fulfilled by finishing up my degree in the city and returning to my hometown, although not as the big man that I have always dreamed of but as someone who could be regarded as an Elite. That alone is worth the feeling. Elites in the out community are always respected and treated like special beings. Now I am moving towards that level, this is really my mother's dream.

I got back into reality by Ali's tap on my knee, on the other side had been enjoying the beautiful sight of the great city and at the same time enjoying the view of the fascinating skyscrapers, prompting him to admire the city.

Our stop is the hotel where we would drop our luggage, freshen up, relax a bit, and then set out later to see the beautiful sight of the city.

"It is pretty going to be fun over here, I have the feels and it's going to set out so well"

I said as I unpacked my bag full of clothes. Looking at the clothes I have on the ground, one would say do I even need any more?

"Yes, pretty fun. I can see beautiful sights right from the second we stepped our foot in here. They are really beautiful places to be and well adorable sights to see." Ali added to my suggestion making it seem like I have a perfect thought and idea.

While we are here enjoying ourselves and at the same time preparing, plans were going on at home and all hands are on deck to make everything come to success. The bride's family has also been putting things in place, ready to see their daughter off and make sure the day is glamorous.

We relaxed a little bit before we could even think of going out. Our journey was pretty stressful. Our room at the hotel seems to be like a room at the penthouse but it isn't. The structure of the hotel on arrival quite got my attention. Makes me wonder what fortune this gigantic building will cost.

Life here makes one dream hugely about oneself and it in a way is such a motivation to almost everyone around. It is also ginger for everyone to work hard. Such is not acquired by lazying around but through hard work and smart work, one would achieve such great feet.

In the evening we set out on seeing some sights and at the same time branch at the nearest supermarket or a mall, whichever we see on our way. We set ourselves out for the shopping.

"Is this what we could call pre-shopping? "Ali asked me jocularly, knowing fully well that we would go on another shopping just tomorrow the day after, to get the major items of clothing and sort.

Our first stop is the grocery store. Ali had reminded me we would be needing some personal items at the hotel.

"Let's get some personal items, not all will be provided at the hotel" he posited to me. I had to concur with him because he's right and we'll be needing them.

Things were cheaper here in Karachi, unlike Islamabad where things are extremely costly which in turn makes the cost and standard of living in such an urban metropolis to be ridiculously high. At a point, it got unbearable for some people especially the people who earn less.

We had the luxury of time to purchase whatever we wanted to in the store and also a pocket full of cash to buy the items. They are quite luxurious but what baffles us is the cheaper prices at which we purchase them.

The storekeeper is a quite jovial lady whose aura of receptiveness describes how well she understands her job description. She attended to us in a manner that prompted Ali and me to engage her in a sound conversation, where she opened up to us that she would love to take a degree in accounting or marketing.

"Quite interesting, you would catch up so easily, considering your deeply rooted knowledge and experience in marketing" I encouraged her in a little way that I could, I tried my best to make her see the positive side of life and how she would be great if she's persistent on whatever she is doing. Ali at the same time was backing me up with his own words too marked by his humorous reactions and his funny comments. I believe if not mostly, the storekeeper enjoyed our little company in their store. My bad, I forgot to ask for her name, it does not matter anyway.

"I believe here will flourish well for businesses and business owners will enjoy their trades quite well over here," Ali said as we later retired to our hotel room.

"Yes, it will, you can see, here is just like a hotspot for Business or what we can call a commercial hub just like other commercial hubs that we read around the world" I added to his submission.

Before arrival, I had heard and read a lot about Karachi being the Industrial and Financial center of Pakistan, little wonder I was not so surprised about the structures of the city. I learned Karachi has the busiest airport in Pakistan. I would love to be there.

The bright ray of light that the curtain ushered in woke us up at the same time. We had a really busy and stressful yesterday hence why we slept so fast and long. We even forgot to eat dinner, that is the extent to which we were tired. I loathe myself out of the bed hitting Ali real well so we could both get up and be set for the day. It is going to be a busy one. We have our day mapped out to be for shopping all the majors we would be needing. And today we would be buying the clothes Ali had made a list for.

After an early morning bath and a warm breakfast of Hot Paratha with Tea. I have it in mind to try out some local Karachi dishes, maybe today or sometimes later. Later might be next year or even a closer date, I do not mind coming here so often, it is nice over here, although I have not spent up to 48 hours in the beautiful city.

Not long into the day, we realize how busy our day would be. We beach to the store where Sherwani was being sold. I was marveled at the beautiful sight before me. I had to check over and over again. Ali who has been. Looking at me all this while having an expression on his face that says everything. The expression of satisfaction.

"I never described this to you, just because I want you to see for yourself, and I am happy you are not disappointed," he said as he also moved closer to me and the beautiful piece. In my mind, I have found a perfect piece of what I am looking for. We bought the beautiful piece not minding the huge money that it costs. That is not even the problem.

We took our time walking down the street checking from store to store, buying our essentials. The wedding is going to be glamorous; I have always thought within myself.

Everything we need is currently on the check, items of clothing for the bride have already been bought. I left that to Ali to choose, which he, in turn, made a real choice, one of the reasons I was excited when he offered to come with me.

We retire later in the evening after a stressful and fun shopping back to our hotel room. There we have to rearrange all that we brought from shopping to easily transport them.

Our item list is not complete because we have not bought the wedding band which people popularly call the wedding Ring. The thought is to go to the port tomorrow to buy it.

I have heard from people that to get fanciful rings in Karachi, the Port is the best place. There you'll have the choice to select from varieties of designs, be it steel, gold, or even diamond. Your answer is at the Port.

CHAPTER THREE

LOST RING

The morning is still very young and vibrant. Ali and I have huge anticipation for the day's activities. I seem hyped for the day and my energy is on a full one hundred percent.

"Positive energy only," I thought to myself as I kickstart the day.

My mind wanders all-around to several events and activities some in the past, some not quite long and some an imagination.

Several pictures are in my head as regards the wedding and I am having a mental picture of the D-day already. Isn't that cute?

Ali on the other hand feeds his sight from the window side. Ali seems to be in love with the city already and the impression he is giving me is quite convincing. His parents never knew he was in Karachi, the only thought on their minds is that their lovely son, my own adorable and best friend is still in Islamabad. They never knew how far their son had gone. The protection of God keeps protecting us and our secrets. This wandered my heart back to how years now, we have kept the secret of our accident in Islamabad from Ali's parents, we never made mention of anything of such to Ali's parents. They actually believe that with me,

Ali is in a quiet safe hand and I would not allow anything evil to happen to him. He definitely is my best friend and I love him so much. I can say he is the mother who never gave to me. I can say that anywhere. Funny how some people took us for blood brothers back in our second year in university.

"You both are all over everywhere together, are you guys brothers?" One had asked at a cafe which I replied positively to.

"Yes we are, brothers, yes" I replied to the fellow and moved on.

I developed the habit of telling these people yes all because I enjoy it when I play on such intelligence. Yes, I take pride in that.

All was set for us to proceed to the activities of the day. All laid out already and we're ready to head out to the port.

"I think it would be better if we could just hire a car for the whole day" Ali suggested to me which I actually at the moment am blank.

"Don't you think the price is going to be exorbitant?" I asked him as soon as I found the right words to utter. His response is quite positive.

"No, it shouldn't, I'll see to that" Ali said assuring me of that fact. Well, everything proved to be positive as we hailed an Uber Cab just at the front of the hotel. Ali as promised catered for that aspect and I got surprised at how he handled it. Just as if he had been in the city for a long time or he was even born in Karachi. He negotiated with the cabbie in a way that the cabbie had no choice but to succumb to Ali's proposal. Ali's Negotiation and bargain prowess could be compared to none, I cherish that part of him so much.

The journey to the port begins and surprises begin to roll in. I guess I have not read so much about this part of Karachi. Just like heaven, the sight before us totally depicts the essence of the city, which is the commercial headquarters of Pakistan. Ranging from industries to corporate entities and other institutes. We later discover that the hospital in which Sidra is having her internship is within that jurisdiction too.

The smooth ride and beautiful sights did not even make us notice how far distance we had covered, because we got carried away by them. In the middle of our journey, we discover that we have covered quite a huge distance and still we keep going. I never journeyed that long even in Islamabad, but here we are having a full exploration of Karachi. It has not been boring since our arrival, funny right?

We need no one to tell us we are at the port premises, before we could decipher that we are there, this is where the deed is getting done, even the blind can tell this.

"This is just too elegant, I guess I have never seen these huge structures before" Ali's voice out after seeing the enormousness s and elegance of these structures. I am excited about this exploration as a part of me feels fulfilled, a kind of dream come through. I come to the conclusion that "I am at where I once dreamt of being to" maybe this does not even make sense to anyone, but it really makes perfect sense to me because I know where I am coming from plus the fact that I am also living my dreams.

We did not get bothered about the store entrance to purchase our beautiful wedding ring. It is quite easy to locate a store that has boldly written for the purpose of the description "Jewelry Store" a store for various expensive pieces of jewelry and gemstones.

"Let us check out that store across, I believe they will have our preferred taste." I signal to the driver while at the same time talking to Ali. The driver halts right at the front of the store. From the exterior, I bet you can say what they sell is luxurious and expensive. We got into the store and what we sight behold is heavenly and divine. Here is a huge store filled with beautiful pieces of jewelry and gemstones ranging from silver to gold and diamonds. These are really what give class and standard to our society. But a rich man's ability to feed others through empowerment is the man of the people. But people tend to love the noise. Preference.

Shopping begins here and we plan to settle for whichever gets my attention, which definitely is not so long to discover.

Sitting pretty at am extreme of the rack is a beautiful silver ring that's shining prompting me to go check it out. As usual, I told Ali about it, and boom we get to check it out and to our utmost surprise, they are cheaper even than what we expected. It is obvious that here in Karachi you have access to so many things. The commerciality of this city depends solely on factors like this and some other related factors too.

We settled for that which we had seen earlier, and I also bought a wristwatch for my bride. Everything we gave to buy in Karachi is getting completed and soon we will be set to get out of here onto the next on our list.

By the time we were done at the store, we both were hungry. Famished just like the word famished. We have been talking about eating one of their local dishes in Karachi and now is an opportunity for us to satisfy our urges and cravings but we would love to still explore this industrial area. We instructed the driver to drive is around here and also take us to one of the best spots in town to get the best of Karachi's delicacy.

"Please you would take us around here and we return outside. Do you know anywhere that we can get local dishes around town?" I instructed him and at the same time made a request?

"No problem, I know of somewhere, but it is quite far from here" the driver replied as politely as he could.

"No issues with the place being far from here," Ali told him as he looked into my eyes to confirm his suspicion, that probably I am reasoning alongside him. Deep down we are quite excited about this as it is going to afford us an opportunity to explore more of the city. And this we never even planned for. That is what they call a two-in-one bag. We secured both.

I have been longing for a taste of some talked about foods and delicacies in Karachi and I feel now is the time to explore each and every one of them. Ali also had for once talked about how hungry he was for Karachi's food and how he cannot wait to devour one.

The driver took us around the port and we could see the majestic doings present at the port. They are so beyond comprehension. The port is the major entrance for foreign goods into Karachi and Pakistan at large. Its major purpose has always been served and the inflow of commodities has never been affected. It is most likely not going to be affected. The creative buildings and structures around the port are deeply in their background cultural heritage. They tell stories that are long in existence, especially about great people who have done so well for humanity. These are just means to immortalize them. They will forever remain in the people's hearts.

Just like the driver had said, we were leaving for a quite far destination, but we had a time that was worth it and at the same time a registered memory.

Our journey to the restaurant seems to be like a rollercoaster of fun and enjoyment. The driver who is now enjoying our company keeps blaring his speaker with some feel-good songs and he even got the vibe along with us, why we said it is quite fun on the road. We are deep into the journey and all that we could see was greatness, different skyscrapers, and beautiful structures all around town.

Then we began moving to the underdeveloped parts of the city. The point that marks a boundary between the expensive neighborhoods and the rural parts is called Saddar Road. The road answered in appropriate ways to the general scaling down in size and structure as it pushed off the rainy area of the city slowly towards the droughty part. The massive buildings of the new rich down the coast gave way to less imposing but still iron roofed and cement walled houses, in much the same way as giant forests of mahogany.

As the car lurched from one side of the road to the other trying to avoid the sharp edges of washed pit bitumen, I noticed that the same iron roofs were now borne more and more on the shoulders of mud walls plastered over with cement. But in due time, this stopped and the walls owned up frankly to being of the reddish heart.

Ali on the other side has a lifted spirit. The lifting of his spirits which had enabled him to indulge himself in every kind of visual and intellectual conceit is due to one great and happy fact. Facts that we have been able to make come true are some of the points on our to-do list, not only the randoms but with a focus on the ones that are preferential and of high importance.

We came by a police post where the policemen at work waved briefly at us.

The car had been traveling for a little over thirty minutes when we got to a famous local market along the roughly tarred road. It is the watering-place of the Great Saddar Road, beloved of the seasoned travelers of the road. It is a chance for us to find fresh air as the driver finds a spot to park.

"This is the market and we will have to go to the restaurant by a leg," the driver says to us as soon as he parks his car under a shed.

The journey to the restaurant also began and it did not take too long to locate the place. It's a restaurant that looks kind of rural from the outside but on getting inside, it is another thing entirely.

An ultramodern interior design and a dining room that is quite serene.

I ordered a plate of Sindhi Briyani while Ali placed an order for Nihari. We ordered a bottle of soft drinks each. The driver also made an order of Briyani too and stepped it down with a bottle of chilled soft drink.

We had a really nice afternoon put there with the food.

We head back to the hotel having in mind that we are meeting with our sister Sidra later in the evening. The journey back to the hotel seems to be faster than the previous journey. We had a smooth ride to the hotel but were quite exhausted and tired. We got to our room and almost immediately we got into this deep sleep but having in the back of our minds that we do not have too much time to sleep, just in less than three hours. They are well not time wasted, but time well spent on the essential elements of our scale of preference. We got ourselves promptly about the timing of our sleep and woke up just briefly.

And now I just got one of the biggest shockers of my life. The beautiful Ring we got at the store could not even be found anywhere near our room. Isn't that insane? In just a twinkle of an eye, we tear down the whole room in search of our beautiful wedding ring. Lots of things to think about at a time and different thoughts going through my head buy how I will be a fine man for the day is the priority. Not being even sure of where I dropped the ring is disturbing.

I went downstairs to the reception just to search for the missing ring and at the same time put in a complaint about my missing ring, so if found, I could be contacted. But I had a doubt in me as regards that and was not even hoping for that, owing to the fact that I am unsure of where I dropped the ring. Could it be in the cab? I asked myself this question, which no one is even there to answer. I am the one responsible for all of this.

The whole situation is becoming disturbing in my head. I could not even make a comprehensive report at the reception. I only had to put myself together and just provide the necessary contact details.

"I would not allow this to ruin my mood," I said to myself just to embrace myself because it is taking a toll on me.

The meeting with Sidra is in the evening and it would be out of count if this in any way comes by my mood.

I cheered myself up with the hope of buying another Ring.

CHAPTER FOUR

SISTER'S WISH

Another opportunity has come upon us today to see and also rejoice with our sister, Sidra. We had earlier contacted Sidra and intimated to her that it's going to be a superb evening of good talks and superb energy. I even told her not to disclose her whereabouts to anyone. To her, this depicts class and pride meanwhile? Be steady on your grind and never let All these bring you down and make it tire you.

The hospital at which she intern avail her not much luxury of time to even get along so well with friends. She has got a really busy schedule which doubles down on he being stressed almost every time. I do not believe the stress is that much until we came to Karachi and we could see things for ourselves, now we know how much our sister works and how tedious the works could be but at this point, this got nothing on her anymore as she has mastered her craft so well to always stay calm even at the middle of the craziest storm. This will help you maintain your mental health and at the same time set you in motion.

After the crazy day, we had from the stress and fun at the port to the fun we had all the way down to the Great Saddar Road where we had our lunch and to the biggest tragedy of them say, misplacing the Beautiful and expensive wedding ring. Deep down I am devastated and sad because this has never been a part of the plan. I will never allow that to disturb my mood and make me become a loner amongst my friends because, on a normal day that is not who I am, it is only the condition that warrants it.

Sidra was beautifully dressed in a silk dress, immediately I spotted that on her I made a huge commentary about how beautiful and gorgeous she looked in the dress.

"Wow, this is superb, I love your dress, you look stunning and beautiful as usual," I remarked

"Thank you, my dear, you have always been the complementing one" she shows gratitude with a blush on her face. That is generally expected of women whenever you compliment them with sweet words, Sidra has always done this so I have taken her to be a perpetual blusher.

"What are you guys ordering? I'm having a bottle of drink" I suggest to them as to light everywhere up and also if not for any other reason but for Sidra. She is quite the one here who needs the most preferential treatment and refreshment.

Just in no time, the attendant rushes down to our table to take our orders. The young lady wearing a uniform whose design represents her as an attendant at such a restaurant. She took into detail all of our orders without mixing them up. She so well manifests her work ethic and the mode of operation. Her swiftness at service is also great, something to actually talk about.

Sidra and Ali are both getting into their usual vibes, throwing shades at each other and making jest of themselves. They can never be caught in, this duo.

"You sure would get you a girl someday" Sidra teased Ali knowing fully well that Ali does not have a girlfriend.

"Get married " Ali on the other hand replies to her in his own expected usual way and also has the knowledge that Sidra will most likely get mad at him but today is quite a good one, she did not fall for Ali's antics this time around. I guess she has learned to always leave Ali to his tantrums because dragging with him leads you nowhere, Ali is only enjoying himself and living the moment. Getting married at this point is not even a priority on Sidra's bucket list. She has quite a long list of goals set to be achieved, getting married now to her seems like a distraction and she can never risk being distracted.

"Marriage is another phase entirely and this phase needs adequate preparation if care is not taken one might lose it" she has always said this in support of her claim and no one ever dispute that with her as that is her opinion and ideology.

In the middle of the talks, Sidra opens up to us about her plan to visit Quetta one of these days.

"I have a plan on going to Quetta one of these days," she says "I need some time out of work" she back herself up. This is just in our usual way of sharing ideas and thoughts, nothing to quite really hold back as we all expressively open up on anything that we have in mind just to free the mind up from all forms of thoughts.

Ali and I have been looking and at the same time, Quetta at the moment is not a good place to be, the level of restlessness in that part is quite on the rise.

"But why Quetta?" I asked her with an expressionless face

"Quetta is not really a safe place at this time and it will be harmful to anyone especially strangers to go there right now "Ali also added. The countenance on Sidra at this moment has changed and I can tell how disappointed she is with just a glance into her eyes.

"No problem, we just can go somewhere else, maybe Hyderabad, one of these days, I just need some time out of here," she said to us as she continues with her own portion of the refreshment.

She remained where she was a long while, till a sudden rebellious rush of ineptitude caused the region of her eyes to swell with the cloudy drizzle of teats tither. I had to deal with that in a measure

We all joked along but I noticed how withdrawn Sidra looks and one could tell she is not happy about the discouragement from going down to Quetta. But the state of things in Quetta is quite unsettled and we cannot risk the danger of going there and becoming a nameless or faceless individual in a community where no one knows me, that will be so unpalatable.

I could read that all the smile she has been putting on is quite fake and she is only doing it to please us and at the same time make is feel-good about ourselves but of what essence.

As it begins to get dark, Sidra excused herself to take her to leave although she does not have a schedule tomorrow she has to leave, according to her.

"I have to leave now," she says, signaling to take her to leave.

"But you do have no schedule tomorrow, why the rush?" Ali Questions her about why she has to leave this early. I on the other hand could decipher what was going on and what even was wrong with Sidra because I could easily read her mood.

She left and we only here talking about random things, the vibe and the energy have already died down all courtesy of the mood with which Sidra left this place. I called Ali's attention to this and trust we will always find a solution to whatever the issue is.

"I think we should go to Quetta, at least satisfy Sidra also" I opined and propose to Ali who in turn show his support towards the course.

"But when do you propose?" Ali asked, this alone shows that he is interested in going to Quetta.

"Why don't you call your father maybe he could give us a car or we find a tour guard, as we both know that Quetta is not a safe place as of this time." I gave another proposition knowing well this can be achieved and it is one of the only ways to safeguard our own security in Quetta.

"You must be kidding me" Ali replies me with a scornful look then continues "my father must not even know I am currently in Karachi or I will be going to Quetta, he will be extremely mad at me," Ali said to me with so much concern but I could not cut him in as I could see he still has lots he wants to talk about.

"Funny you, my father is not even the Minister" he continues, "to be dolling out exotic cars to his erring son," Ali said as he laughs hysterically "He would kill me and you if he knows we are in Karachi together and that we are planning to go to Quetta together, you'll be gone man" He submitted jokingly and we laughed it over knowing fully well that way is a no go.

We talk a little more before standing to leave. We make our way out and just shortly after a brief walk through the walkway, we heard a voice from behind us making quite a huge loud voice from behind us, which seems like someone is running towards us. The pace is accompanied by the voice saying "Hey, you guys cannot do this, stop there. Hey! Hey!!!!......"

Ali looked at me and says discreetly "Let us run, I think this guy is from Quetta" he might be right, we have said pretty much bad about Quetta in the restaurant and if someone from Quetta is in the restaurant, he would want to retaliate. He might be one of those dangerous guys. We both took to our heels but we got cut short by huge security guards who hit us to the ground.

"What have we done to you?" I question the guy who held on to me as his life depends really on it.

Ali on the other hand was dragging with the huge security guy that pin him down to the ground, but the guy overpowered him. He landed Ali on the Ground which made the guy be on top of him. Ali scampered to breathe so hard.

The manager who was running after us earlier says we wanted to abscond from the restaurant without paying

"They bought something from us and wanted to leave without paying up" he alleged.

It was a mistake on our part, we got carried away by the thoughts of our next adventure and planning.

We apologize to them and Ali make payment for everything that we had purchased, which he even add extra cash to. We make sure we settle everything with them at the restaurant before leaving for our hotel.

We have been trying our very best not to get into any trouble with anyone, if not for me, for Ali whose parents do not even know he is in Karachi with me. I have to put everything in order.

The journey back to our hotel took like an eternity as everything seem boring to us.

We could not even secure a cab on time and it seemed like forever to even stop one or get one to convey us down to the hotel.

At last, we journey down to our hotel and it looks like we are going to be on the road for life.

Ali has been dozing off right from the car, it almost looked like I dragged him all the way to our room upstairs.

"Not like I am drunk man, I can walk," Ali said sleepily as we head towards our room. One thing Peculiar to him is how serious he takes his sleep and his leisure, they are things he does not play or joke about. He gives premium attention to these two things because he thinks they are the mechanisms to living a quiet good life. He believes nothing should disrupt or disturb his sleep and he has always respected this when it comes to people.

Ali went straight on to the bed as soon as we got to our room, "he needs to sleep" I thought to myself, and in no time, he's fast asleep, peaceful and calm just like a baby.

I have little things to go over and I will not be going to bed soon.

The thought of the lost ring just struck my heart and I am back to being sober and calm. I try reflecting on how I had misplaced the magical piece. I thought real much about it trying to trackback my steps from the store to everywhere that we had touched down.

"Where could it have been?"

"Did I not just lose my wedding ring?

These are the questions popping up in my head, making me reason too much about how far I have come in this journey to have lost this such rare stone. I got to a point where everything seems just so tiring to me, I could not even wrap my head around the whole happening, this brings me to the question "why is this happening to me at this period?" This question is not meant for anyone but my own psychology, it actually is a test on my mental and now I just failed my own question.

The anger and tiredness that came with the frantic searching of the lost ring lands me in a deep sleep and I launched myself into it trying to drive myself away from the realities of my wor and sadness, I slept off on this and could not sleep for so long.

At around 2 AM in the morning I opened my eyes from the quick sleep that I just had. The sleep was quite helpful as it relieves me a little bit from all the emotional pieces of baggage that cluster my mind. I really have to free my mind, from all these pieces of baggage maybe I will even remember where I dropped the ring.

Opening my eyes quite a little bit, I could see Ali sitter by the window side with a glass of water in his hands and him tying his robe around himself, looking over the street like he's employed to do so or he's some night watchman. As I noticed he's awake I decide to reignite the discussion going to Quetta and at the same time make a final decision on it, which would be better if we could go to Quetta just to fulfill our sister's wish and desire plus it is part of the exploration.

"What do you have in thought about a trip to Quetta?" I asked Ali firmly trying to ascertain his own stand and opinion so we would not be left in the lurch and the sane time would know the next line of action.

"I am of the opinion that we should go, no matter what the impediment could be" he gave his own piece of inspiration.

We agreed on going to Quetta and also bringing Sidra along with us.

We made use of our hotel land-phone to place a call through to Sidra whom we believe might still be asleep but we need to put this call to her to let her know the state of our mind on it.

"Hello," she said in her croaky voice as one can tell she is fast asleep "why are you guys in my dream?" she says jokingly in her manner. She never lost her vibes, not even for once while asleep.

"We would be going to Quetta tomorrow" we inform her

"Wow, so what changed your mind?" She asked inquisitively

"At 8:00 AM let's make breakfast together tomorrow and then plan on how we will get to Quetta either by bus or by train". I told her in an affirmation tone just to make her sure that we are pretty serious about our decision.

"No problem, see you in the morning, but stop appearing in my dream you two".

We rounded off the whole conversation on a happy note and I am excited that we got Sidra to smile. And that we all have something to actually laugh and giggle out loud about.

CHAPTER FIVE

UNKNOWN PLACE

The fresh morning dew that greets the cold morning brings with it a refreshing taste. After what seemed like a horrid yesterday. The whole day was literally what explains the word stressful, coupled with the horrible incident of the lost wring. I still could not wrap my head around the fact that such a beautiful and expensive ring is gone. I cannot even ascertain where to trace or track it towards. I resigned go fate.

A busy day ahead which we do not know the turn this would take. Journey to Quetta, where we have never been to. Sounds scary and even uncertain. At the moment, we do not even know the safest route to Quetta as we have been deliberating on whether to go via bus or by train. In my thoughts, going by train would worsen the situation as we do not know for the city is and the train itself would even take time.

It was around 6 AM when we woke up from our brief sleep after calling Sidra to get herself prepared for the journey ahead of us. I literally had a little sleep after then and the same thing goes with Ali. I still feel drowsy but I dare not sleep.

"Your eyes are heavy and you look just so sleepy," Ali says after paying just too close attention to me and knowing well that my lids are sleepy too.

I had already packed every one of our things overnight while Ali was asleep and at the same time I had everything in place but the thought of the lost ring clouded my mind so much that I hate myself for getting it lost.

"I would buy another one, maybe finer," I thought to myself in consolation. I have it in mind to purchase another ring since the wedding is still in more days. By then I would get money to purchase a finer and even more expensive ring. This has been my thought so well.

Ali and I set out for breakfast at the same venue we told Sidra to meet with us. She had already been there, awaiting our arrival and as expected, we definitely default the time.

"Perpetual latecomers," she says as Ali and I take our seat opposite her. She knows us to always be late to whatever it is, only if it concerns Ali and me alone.

We had a quick breakfast and we were all set for the station to file our travel ticket to Quetta. Deep down we all have this mixed feeling within us but still had to keep going. The tough thought in you pushes you to do the unimaginable.

The booking office is just a thirty minutes drive from our hotel. We had a quite smooth ride to the station and this time around in a more comfortable ride, bidding Karachi a grand goodbye, although I have plans to come back in the nearest future.

I never knew Ali's plan on whether to come back or not. All that I am sure of me is I would come back. For the last time before we leave this beautiful city, we admire the architectural designs and structures erected by world-class engineers.

The Bus station is not as pretty as expected. Here is a crowded station with sweaty people all around and people everywhere waiting for the next turn.

We got to the ticket point and we met another disappointment. Aside from the stuffy room where several people were stuck, the attitude of the attendant is also not a good one. He has a handful of tickets but was partially attending to people who have been on the queue.

I inquired about buses going from Karachi to Quetta and got the shocker of my life.

"Quetta buses leave in the evening" the old man responds with passive attention.

I wonder in my mind why would bus going from Karachi to Quetta leave in the evening? A journey this far would be embarked on at night? I had to keep my fears to myself as I did not in any way want to discourage my friends. The expression on their face seems to be nothing short of the one I just had on mine. Ali I believe would calm Sidra down or vice versa, any which way.

Now we have to wait from this morning till evening, such a long hour, then we will journey between seven and nine hours. That is pretty breathtaking and very exhausting and time-taking. The question now is what to do till the bus would take off in the evening. We all have our tickets intact in our pockets, ready to hit the road whenever it is time.

I could see a mixed mood in Sidra who has relaxed on one of the long benches in the station. She is quite excited and in anticipation of what our journey holds and at the same time may be scared of the danger that the journey holds and also, we are going into a land where no one knows us and at the same time we are unknown and unrecognized.

"Are you scared?" I asked her at the slightest opportunity

"Scared of what?" She asked as she looked blankly into my eyes, she was lost for the first few seconds, trying to find the best words to utter and all that she could utter was the question.

"Maybe the journey" Ali cuts in, I never knew Ali was being attentive to what I have been telling her, I was surprised by his contribution because he seemed engrossed in the newspaper he was reading.

"Maybe I am, but I am excited and curious too," she says as she takes a little break to take in some air. "You know I have never been to Quetta and I have been longing to be there. I do not know what to expect, maybe positive or negative, but we get there first." She concludes. This fact brought in strength for everyone and our interest in exploring Quetta was on the increase and we got the vibe again.

The time seems to be in a slowing mode and everything seems to be drawing like the snake. It looks like it is taking an eternity. Ali is the first person to complain of hunger. He had been trying to hide the feeling but not any longer. He is not the only one battling with that feeling as I am also feeling the pangs of hunger in my tummy, my stomach rumbles and I can't help but also support my dear friend in the struggle.

"Seems the worms in my stomach are clamoring for a refill" Ali voiced out as hunger hits him harder.

"Do not tell me you are hungry" I said in return trying to find a better placement for my words.

"He is more than hungry, he can devour a whole cow," Sidra says jokingly as she tries to buttress how hungry Ali is because she knows him just like the back of her hand.

We finally settled to eat one of the numerous snacks being displayed by traders at the station, 'Kurkury' that is the name. The taste is superb and I would love to have more by the way. We bought more to get something edible that is going to sustain us for the journey because it is going to be a long evening.

At exactly 5 PM, buses on the Quetta route began to gather in the arena to transport passengers to Quetta and her neighboring cities.

Your ticket is your pass into the bus en route to Quetta and we would not be making the mistake of getting the tickets lost.

We are lucky to secure our seats closer to ourselves and the view here would enable us to have our usual endless chats and clatters, plus the feeling that comes with journeying side by side with your loved ones. The long bus that I estimated to contain almost fifty passengers at a time began to fill up and in just the twinkle of an eye, the bus got filled up to the brim with both passengers and their heavy luggage and big bags.

"All passengers on board, the trip is about to start" this was the tiny female voice that ran through the station on a loud mic just to announce to the passengers that buses are about to take off and everyone should be ready to take off too. It is quite surprising to see some of the supposed passengers scamper all around just to secure their seats on a bus, meanwhile, we have the luxury of two hours earlier to do this, but some had gone to the restroom to ease themselves while some went to buy edibles and some are just perpetual latecomers,

At exactly 7 PM the buses took off one after the other leading themselves towards the same direction. It is getting a bit dark as the sun tends to set early nowadays.

The journey begins and we are some hours and kilometers away from Quetta.

We did not have a journey quite eventful enough to be talked about. What is excoriated about the rough road that leads to Quetta in the middle of the night? What fun comes with going to Quetta in this kind of condition.?

Ali and I intermittently look at each other with fear written all over our faces.

Out of curiosity, Ali had asked

"Are we going to die?"

This shows the level at which Ali is scared

"We are not going to die" I replied trying to allay his fear but at the same time, fear is boldly showing in my voice.

I would hold Sidra's hands intermittently to show her that all is going to be well and fine.

She also asked me "will this be our last trip?" She asked me out of fear as we go deep into the thick dark part of the night.

"Should we inform our parents about this?" I asked out of curiosity and the fact that I can't find the right words to say.

"Are you high? what are will we call our parents, do you want to kill us?" Ali counters my opinion of calling our parents as he frowns completely at it. I had no choice but to withdraw from my shell.

"The best thing is to die away from your family," he said summing all his talks up.

These are quite the questions of fact-checking and reasonability. Throughout the journey was quite on his toes and could not even get his own eyes to sleep. The journey of almost twelve to fifteen hours in the middle of nowhere, we all have to keep our watch, but some people still were able to sleep in the middle of these all night, there's a man behind me who slept all through the night and snored all through, this middle-aged man could not even keep awake for few hours into the journey before he drifted to the dreamlands and forgot that he is on a midnight journey to the land where he is unknown, instead, he is supposed to be extra-vigilant and careful.

At exactly 4 AM, the bus halted and it seemed like it had reached where everyone would alight at our destination. Directly opposite this spot is a huge signpost that reads "Welcome to Quetta" I took my time to check around the environment if it is safe for us at an early time of the morning.

Everywhere is safe and on the check but where do we go from here? How on earth do we even locate a hotel in this place when it is even still dark.

We're welcome to Quetta as the cold that greeted us on arrival was huge, enormous, and quite unbearable.

Geographically, Quetta is at -2'C, how cold is this city? This depicts the quite cold natural tendency of the city of Quetta. This is the definition. The major factor that contributes so much to this is the fact that this is January, it is the period of harmattan but we do not have on us a cover cloth or a sweatshirt.

We are only left with the choice of wandering and loitering around because we could not even get a vehicle or even a hotel where we could lodge before the start of the day. "Isn't it dangerous and harmful for strangers who know nowhere to go or where to turn to when dangers come" this and a whole lot of thoughts clustered in my mind at the moment? This in return clouded my reasoning as I could not even come by any solution to our present predicament. True is the ideology that says that the problem is only five percent and how you approach or tackle it makes up the remaining ninety-five percent. This in return would make or mar the aftermath of such a predicament.

He thus beheld in the pale morning light the resolve to separate the good from the bad, not as a hot and indignant instinct, but denuded of the passionateness which had made it scorch and burn; standing in its bones, nothing but a skeleton, but there.

As we keep wandering, we came by a bus connector whom we engaged and asked if we could secure a hotel room around here and we got one of the greatest revelations on this journey

"Where are you and where are you going to? He asked trying to be certain of the faces before him.

"We are coming from Karachi and we are here but we are looking for a hotel to lodge" Ali responds trying his possible best to be as calm as possible because we do not know how real this person is and we are new here, we would not want to get ourselves into troubles and problems that will involve the police or the authorities.

"You are in Quetta man, this is too early for hotels to be open, not quite safe out here," the short bald man said to us. Funny how I could notice he is bald despite the tense condition that is on the ground. The man explained to us how things work in Quetta and where not to go.

From the way he talks, one could tell that he is a quite nice man. He talks passionately but our fear has still not been allayed.

He propose to us that he has a shop around the corner and that we could come stay at his shop if we do not mind. We were at first skeptical about it and had to think so well about it.

"Please give us a little time "I pleaded with the man.

"Should we trust this man?" Sidra asked as she looks at the man viciously with a look that suspicion is written all over.

"How do we know? We just met him" I replied. How do we know if someone whom we just met is a good person?

"let us just try our leap of faith, not like we have any other place to put up till daybreaks" Ali suggests and I at the same time reasoned with him on this, we need a place to at least keep our heads till its daybreak.

We accept to follow this man to his said shop just to stay till its morning.

He leads the way to the shop just as dark as the morning seems to be, meanwhile, we follow him with full consciousness of our environment trying to figure out if there's anything wrong or not because we do not want to become victims of circumstance.

He brought us to the said shop which is quite close to the bus station. The shop does not in any way look like his and also it looks empty, just like there has been no activity in the shop. As we noticed this, Ali and I signal to each other and I can sense the uncomfortable look that is on Sidra's face.

The man told us he would be leaving us at the shop and that he needs to join them at the station as we all know he is a bus conductor.

"I would be back soon, let me get back to the bus station" he pleads so we can excuse him for his daily job, not like he is even going to be responsible to us about the work or proceeds.

He left us in the shop and went ahead with his daily hustle.

As soon as he left, I gave my premium attention to the shop, observing and examining the way things are, how the shop looks empty and I could say it doesn't fit for what we can call a standard shop, no wares, nothing, just a space. I looked further around the shop and I discover something strange, scary and really bad. At first, I thought I was hallucinating but no I am right. I saw a very bot knife under the bench that is directly opposite us and to complement it, some few bloodstains around. To confirm my suspicion I alert Ali who was not even sleeping but also observing.

"Seems the end has come," I said to Ali as I tried as much as possible to contain my fears.

I stylishly point to the big knife and Ali sprang up like he's about to pick a race.

I never knew Sidra was also paying closer attention or she just saw it. She screamed out loud and we all got terrified.

"God please Save us" she prays to God.

"What's wrong?" Ali asked her.

She could not utter a word, she's only team line which got Ali and me terrified the more.

I discretely follow the path of her eyes and I got another thing that requires the immediate evacuation of the shop. It is a white cloth stained with blood.

We had to assure ourselves that all was going to be well and that we would scale through this.

Now several questions are in our minds, are we safe? We should run, that is the only answer.

We took to our heels in search of safety and security. We met our waterloo after we walked for like five minutes. The cold started becoming unbearable for us, we did not take along with us our sweatshirt. We scampered and scavenged for safety, the safety of our lives, and also against cold.

We couldn't even find it anywhere.

"Should we call our parents?" Sidra asked again but I shunned that idea.

"We do not have any other option than to go back to where we are coming from, once again with good faith," I said, appealing to them. Ali is freezing already and he needs a cover. I had to cover him up with one of the clothes we brought from Karachi.

We all agree to go back to the shop.

Thank goodness we could trace our steps back and locate where the shop is. We decided not to enter but stayed right at the front.

The time is moving unlike before, but we still couldn't find a hotel.

Not quite long after we settled down, the stranger man appeared from the dimmed light. We sprang up to our feet like we were about to run but he calmed us down.

"Guys, do not be afraid" he pleaded.

"Thank you, we are fine, but no we are not staying" Ali harshly replies.

"I am a very good and calm guy, I can do you no harm" he convinces us with his words. We had to stick together because of the cold.

We deliberated on what to do and we're uncertain enough. During our deliberation, our little host was on a phone call with an indistinct caller. The crux of their discussion is unknown and at the same time, we're scared.

Once again, the thought of calling our parents strolled in but it was immediately discarded as it's a no-go area.

Should we call the police? How do we even go about that now?

We just have to leave as it's even about an hour to morning, when we can comfortably sort for a hotel.

Just as we are about to take off, the stranger called on us that he had a piece of good news for us.

"Hey, good news!" He says and then continues after a brief stop.

"I just arranged a home for you guys, come with me to my house," he says. This strange man here who has been our host just offered us his own home, to stay. We look at ourselves with different thoughts running through our heads, but I guess we are waiting on who is going to speak first.

Sidra is the first person to get her tongues together. "Thank you for your kind gestures and hospitality, but we would pass, we are going to get a hotel, thank you," she says as one can see the fear in her voice.

Our stranger host, who seemed to have noticed the fear in her voice tries to calm her down and make her be at peace.

"I understand your fears my sister, but I can assure you that you are safe with me. I have a daughter and sister like you, so I can do you no harm. I have also talked to my mother about this and she has agreed to it" he says as he tries to convince us more. "and I don't think you guys can get a hotel around now" he added.

Inside of me, I am a bit convinced but not totally, and I believe the same as Ali which prompted him to ask about the stained cloth and the long knife.

"And what is it with the long knife and stained cloth?" The stranger bursts into laughter and could not even restrict himself as he laughs uncontrollably. And hysterically.

"Oh, that?. It belongs to my father, he is the owner of this shop and he is also a butcher. You do not have any reason to fear, I am a good person" he says.

As soon as he said this, he felt a huge relief on us, and just like a burden had just been removed from us, we still have to discuss this among ourselves in such a way that we do not run into any trouble in this strange land.

"Please, excuse us, we need to talk," I said to the stranger in such a way that he doesn't feel disrespected.

We deliberated amongst ourselves whether to follow the strange man to his place or not. Ali suggests that we follow him since he's a good person and also we can't find a hotel, his place would suffice as a hotel and also he is not a complete stranger because he is from the bus station and he is traceable. We concluded that we would be going to his house but for a really short while.

"We are going to follow you to your place, but we will be spending a little time". I said to him, making him understand my plight and ploy to stay over at his abode.

CHAPTER SIX

I'M SORRY

Everything here seems to be calm, not up to that of Karachi, but less of what has been heard of Quetta. Our host is playing a superb role in getting us the best nicely treatment he could (in his own capabilities because he is not responsible for us).

He treated us to a nice breakfast in the morning just as soon as we got to his abode.

His aging mother is also receptive to us, accommodating a sweet old lady. She took Sidra in just like hers and also treated Ali and me like we were his sons.

Our thought was to stay over at the man's place till evening with the thought of surprising Sidra's friend. Sidra before we left Karachi had told us that her friend is in Quetta and that we might be staying over at hers and she would also be able to guide us through Quetta. Although I personally did not put all my hope on that, still rooting for better options to make our visit to Quetta a memorable one.

In the end, we still got disappointed in this. Sidra put a call through to her friend Sanaya and one could tell from the conversation that the outcome was just one of the negative responses one gets. I looked at Ali who seemed not to physically pay attention, but my friend was attentive to the last detail of the conversation.

"Where do we go from here?" She asked just after dropping the call. And now we know we're in it.

"My friend Sanaya and her family are not in town and they will not be back soon" she breaks the not so sad news to us.

"I am sorry Sidra, she says soberly" There is of course no point in being sorry or sober. The plan is to surprise her friend but now, it could not work out and we have to devise a strategy, A plan B.

She remained where she was for a long while, till a sudden rebellious rush of ineptitude caused the region of her eyes to swell with the cloudy drizzle of teats tither.

The reality just dawned on me that we have no one to run to, only that we get a hotel or if it is possible we stay at our hosts' but we never knew his thoughts. The best thing now is to stay here with The stranger man who has turned to our host.

To an extent, this place is not bad, beautiful, and nice people. His mother has been a very sweet woman since our arrival. She had taken Sidra just like a daughter and also treated Ali and me as her sons.

Ali and I are to stay in the guest room and Sidra would stay with the old lady. The family has really been a sweet one to us and we're taken care of just like children in the house.

Bit by bit, we are getting quite relaxed with the family and things are going just the way they are supposed to be.

The old lady and Sidra and having a really good time together and I can say it is quite sweet to see them together in this kind of scene.

I had called on Sidra once to ask how relieved she is about being here for the time being, in a strange land without father nor mother.

"I am beginning to like it here," she said and continued after a short pause " it is quite fun with the old lady, she's loving and caring, she's got a tender feeling" she added, making me feel relaxed about her safety and security. Also, I could not ask any further questions.

She at the same time took me through rounds of incidents that had happened to prove that the woman was who she claimed she was. Just within a little while, they could get so well together to the extent that she told Sidra about Quetta. Things that we never knew about Quetta and its environs.

From what Sidra told me, I could say that Quetta had been a really great city and an influx of tourists was on the rise in this great city until things went south. With numerous notorious activities perpetrated by bandits which include kidnapping, raiding, and stealing. This got tourists from far-away places across the world, places like Africa.

All these are what make everything in Quetta come together and be one in just one accord. Local businesses in Quetta are the most flourishing around town.

The standard of living in Quetta then was not as exorbitant as now. Everything has increased in price sporadically and the least of people in society began to struggle just to make ends meet.

Our host and his mother belong to this set of people in society, but they always try their best to be a really good host to us and we also try to put up our best behavior, not forgetting the fact that they are our own God sent helper.

Ali and I in the way to show support would help in cleaning the house and at the same time put things in order just the way they are supposed to be.

The bus conductor on the other hand would go to work. He is solely a major figure in the family. He fends for the family's needs and wants, such a responsible young man.

We both had a quick smooth conversation on a bright evening where we talked about the disadvantages of not being able to provide for ourselves.

"I once had nothing on me, I was at my most broke," he said trying to explain his predicament while he had no money at all. "My mother tried her best at raising us so well. She at least gave us the best life that she could afford, despite the fact that things are hard and not easy to get by.

"What about your father?" I asked inquisitively. "You barely talk about him" I added.

"My father lives far away from the city," he says before he continues "I took you to his shop the first day we met. He is a butcher." He explains. He barely talks about his father and anytime he does, he keeps it so brief and short.

Ali is also getting along and everywhere is getting good, no issues just good energy and vibes.

Sidra has become quite attached to the old lady and I feel so happy about that. The essence of our coming to Quetta was not a failure after all.

Her fascination grew as she explored with her wife's amazing eyes the wonderful land. I find her freshness quite appealing. Now she nudges Ali and points at the legends inscribed on the wall of the bar raised above.

We all have a role or more to play which must play and adapt so well.

We have to put up here for the time being. We do not really know how long it is going to be but we keep hoping it does not take longer than we expect.

We all could see how well we get along with people. They show us massive love in their own capability. The one they could show and would never want to harm us.

Sidra was still a bit nursing the guilt she felt earlier when she called her friend.

"You do not have to be moody because of that," I said to her when I noticed she was down and all was as a result of her friend not being in town

She has a fragile heart which I personally would not want to be damaged because as fragile as it is, it is extremely beautiful. What a loving soul.

CHAPTER SEVEN

WHERE TO NOW

In just a little space of given time, a lot has happened. Our stay in Quetta has been quite an experience, a rollercoaster of different feelings, right from the first minute at the bus station to the activities that follow.

No gainsaying, our stay with them has really enhanced our horizon and at the same time, we have learned quite some things about Quetta, the people, and how things work over there.

We're having quite enough fun, if not more than enough that we could say it is an adventure. An adventure into a land where people, especially foreigners do not visit just because of the previous bad records and the bad name given to the city.

Our host had once taken us to the amusement parks around Quetta. Some were a bit scanty, the situation of things in town has not really allowed people to come all out to have fun. All these are due to social degeneration and moral decay. Hence, why we were afraid when we touch down Quetta. The fear of the unknown is due to several past incidents and some fresh most recent awful incidents.

The old lady is fond of telling us different scenarios of the crisis years even before now. The implication of these scenarios has been immense on the growth of the community. It shaped and at the same time balanced.

The scarcity of food and farm produce in Quetta could not be talked about without discussing the effects of the Earthquakes on the development of the city.

The Earthquake has been one of the greatest environmental problems that has been battling Quetta for a long time. There are vast and immense negative effects on the economy and other aspects of life due to this. This disaster crippled numerous commercial activities not only in Quetta but in neighboring areas and communities. Quetta is the tenth largest city in Pakistan, and it used to hold a huge pillar of the Pakistan economy. Quetta till now has been a bedrock of farming and fruits cultivation.

Before this time, trees had become hydra-headed bronze statues so ancient that only blunt residual features remained on their faces, like anthills surviving to tell the new grass of the savannah about last year's brush fires.

Household animals were all dead. The sheep and goats and cattle choked by their swollen tongues. Stray dogs in the marketplace in a running battle with vultures devoured the corpse of the madman they found at last coiled up one morning in the stall over which he had assumed unbroken tenancy and from where he had sallied forth every morning to mount the highest rung of the log steps at the center of the square and taunt the absent people.

Even the clouds were subdued though they had held out longest. Their bedraggled bands rushed their last pathetic resources from place to place in a brave but confused effort to halt the monumental formations of the sun's incendiary hosts. For this affront, the sun wreaked a terrible vengeance on them cremating their remains to their last plumes and scattering the ashes to the four winds. Except that the winds had themselves fled long ago. So the clouds' desecrated motes hung suspended in a mist across the whole face of the sky and gave the sun's light glancing off their back the merciless tint of bronze. Their dishonored shades sometimes would stir in the futile insurrection at the spirit hour of noon starting a sudden furious whirling of ash and dust, only to be quickly subdued again.

Our thoughts began to reach a clandestine, questions began to pop up in our heads, not knowing what answers to feed them with.

"Are we going to be here for long?" I once asked myself out of deep thought into discovering inwardly, the next line of action.

Ali on the other hand had sunk into resigning to fate and flow with how things turn out from here.

Sidra on her own is enjoying her good company with the old lady and this looks like Quetta is becoming a good space for her. All her fears have been allayed and she now feels so much at home and not concerned anymore about whether the whole place is safe or not. In my own thoughts, I believe she just found peace in the Quetta or this is the fulfillment of why she has been so hungry to come to Quetta. Quite a place for her.

"I have been wanting to take quite a little break away from work and all the stress and problems of it" she once revealed to me how fulfilled she is to be in Quetta. I could feel the zeal and passion in her voice. The urge to see more of Quetta is there still in her, the spirit of exploration

"Not to worry, we would take a tour pretty around the city, that would be a quite well experience "I had proposed to her in a way that she would definitely be interested in going with us.

Ali on his own part had been on the jump to any of my offers, we both know how we work things out together and I am not in any surprise at how things turned out to be.

"Is this how things are going to continue?" Ali asked me after a short rest in the guest room. This seemed to me like a parable and I would want him to speak to me in a language that I understand so well.

"I do not understand your insinuation, would you stop speaking in parables?" I posited to him as a child not even grasping the crux of his question.

"What I am saying, in essence, is that, is this how we will continue here? Where do we go from here, what is our next plan of action, because this is not our home and we cannot stay here for too long, we need to device a means just to get out of here" Ali cries out, speaking passionately about this, I know how disturbed and worried his mind could be at the moment. His parents never knew where he was, now should he leave himself hanging in the air here in Quetta where he knows no one"

These are thoughts crazy enough to drive even me nuts but I had to steady my emotion in such a way that it does not affect one.

The question on where to go next from here resounds in my own head too, I want to voice out my opinion too, but who is going to listen to me rant on them, I bet no one. But I had to allow Ali to voice out his grievances, it's eating him up, it'll be of courtesy if I could calm him down and bring his head below the heat level.

At this point, a renewed sense of questioning had risen up in me and I had withdrawn to attend to it. Why am I still here? Obviously, the reason that had first offered itself might have to do with being here by mistake or just on purpose. None really fits into this, owing to the fact that everything is happening one after the other.

"Firstly, we are not going to be here for too long" I assured him before continuing with my own talks "The point is this, we just can stay here a little and then back to Tharparkar," I told him outrightly and I could see he subscribes to the idea.

"I understand you brother, I am just a bit bothered and perturbed at how things turn out and the fact that the bus connector is our savior " he added just to buttress my point and opinion.

Later in the evening, we had a brief walk around and a little talk erupts about the observation Sidra has made as regards the people of Quetta

"The people here are quite hyperactive and conscious of every danger that could be looming" she noted as we walk briskly down the muddy road "they tend not to be friendly to strange faces" she concluded.

Yes, she is right. The people here are quite less friendly all owing to their past experience. I realized this not long ago, the actual earlier the better. It is just wonderful how our host had taken us in without hesitation. Such a kindhearted man.

There is a need for us to equally map out the course at which our journey is going to take so as not to lose traction of everything. We still have quite a number of belongings in Karachi which need pickup. I thought In my mind that Ali would be able to do that.

CHAPTER EIGHT

COLD AND QUETTA

The extremely cold weather in Quetta says nothing about the city but the fact that it shows how core West northern the old city is.

We have had a series of encounters with the cold humidity, right from our first morning in Quetta.

"Everyone here knows the drill, you have to kit really up to beat the coldness here," our host told us this when we noticed we could not hold it anymore and we were without a sweater or sweatshirt to prevent the penetration of the cold. That was the first morning when we would feel this, with the thoughts that the following days would be better. Little did we know that we were only deceiving ourselves and at the same time sparking a false hope from within.

The meads were beginning to change, but it was still warm enough in early afternoons for milking to idle there awhile, and also the state of things at this time

The cold distressed Ali more than it would have done had he been with a sweater or cardigan. With a feeling of faintness, he retired back into the room which I followed suit just to ensure that he is fine and well. He looked a little disturbed, I thought. He said not a word to me in the room, indirectly signifying how intense this is and unless he subjects himself to intensive care and thank goodness. Sidra knows well much about this. She would be able to decipher Ali's current state.

"He is only reacting to the cold weather, it is really nothing serious or to worry about" these words of Sidra calmed me down so well and it even diffused tension in the whole house. He took some cold relief pills which Sidra herself had bought at the nearest pharmacy which made him sleep so well.

Just like magic, everything worked out so well in a short while. Ali got up just like nothing had happened to him before or he was not the one shivering some few hours ago.

"I feel so relieved, just like a burden got lifted," Ali remarked just immediately when he woke up.

There in my mind is a leap of joy that my friend is back on his feet as himself again. At least we do not have any course to say we would have to be at the hospital, because that on its own is a long way.

"I heard Ali had a cold in the morning, " our host asked me as soon as he got back from work

"Yes, he did. He is better now" I responded to him just to assure him of his safety.

"I would say you should go to the market tomorrow. You definitely would be able to buy a cardigan or sweater for future purposes too" he advised. The piece of advice he gave was quite good just so one can know. We all need a cardigan in this weather especially in this part of the country, where if care is not taken one would put a bucket full of water out in the cold and it will all freeze up.

"Come and buy from me" was the buzzing sound of market traders at the big market in Quetta.

We had come out to get some of our personal essentials. Our host, the bus connector had described to us how to get to the market and at the same time the spot to get what we need to buy.

The top on our priority list is to buy cardigans if not for the three of us, but Ali. It was not hard before we could locate a stall where they sell all varieties of cardigans and sweatshirts. This avail is the opportunity to select the ones of our choice and preference. A thick black female hood got my attention which I bought with the intention of gifting my bride with such beauty.

"It is a bit hard over here to get all that you have mentioned at retail outlets on the streets, you have to get to the market to buy all those" he advised us on a morning when we needed some personal essentials which include soaps, shaving items amongst others. Sidra also needs some more items for herself, this brings us with no choice other than to go to the market to source for all these items.

We left for the market quite early in the morning to beat all the hurdles of the market. We still were unable to get through the teeming crowd which seemed to be like a troop or legion.

We had finished buying the items we came to the market to purchase, Ali and were headed home to deliver what we bought to Sidra and the old lady so they can both fix them up and also make some food for the whole house. The family has quite been nice to us as regards feeding, the old lady has always made sure that we are well fed, the bus connector also did his best in getting us the best of refreshments in Quetta, all ate on our own funds and title.

Food in Quetta is not as expensive as we thought it would be. Quetta being a bedrock for food and farm produce gave us the opportunity to explore more of the produce cultivated on the lands of Quetta.

We know how much energy these people put into cultivating and how much they end up selling their produce. The prices are almost close to being ridiculous. This shows in how they run the market system in Quetta.

One of the most cherished virtues is appreciation. Every now and then if not spoken, I appreciate our host in my heart, who never made us feel like we are outcasts. He never knew us from nowhere but still decided to help us out, despite the present situation of things in town.

Towards noon, the weather had changed and the cheers on people's faces could be seen from the rearview. Ali on his own had been out of the cold plus we had made reservations for the cold weather. It comes that way.

Now that we know Ali's nature, it is easier to say and do than to just say alone. Leaving one at the mercy of the weather is quite detrimental as it could with any other ailment.

The encounter with Ali came at a very early moment, one of all moments calculated to permit its impact with the least trauma and shock. But such was an unreasoning memory that, although he stood there openly and palpably, fear overcame him, paralyzing the movement so that he neither moves forward nor backward.

To now think about what emanated from his countenance when he saw this, and to even behold the sight of it is quite a lot of rigor. This was the same handsome pleasant man, but then the look he wears is quite unwelcoming.

The measure which we took to fight the said cold is more traditional and these means are quite not ridiculous.

Then one day, a peculiar quality invaded the air of the whole house. There came a moisture which was really not from rain, and such cold was not from frost. It chilled the eyeball of the twain, made their brows ache, penetrated to their skeletons, affecting the surface of the body less than its core. They knew all that it meant, it meant snow, and it came in the night. The Emperor during this period had resorted to staying in the cottage with the warm gable that cheered any lonely walker who paused beside it, awoke in the night, and heard above the thatch noises which seemed to signify that the roof had itself turned into a gymnasium of all the winds. When he lit up his lamp get up in the mornings, he found that snow had blown through a chink in the casement, forming a white cone of the finest powder against the inside and had also cone down the chimney, so that it lay sole deep upon the floor, on which his shoes left tracks when he moved about. Without, the storm drove so fast as to create a snow-mist in the kitchen; but as yet it was too dark outdoors to see anything.

The house was rid of persons at this time. Ali was reading his journals as usual and would take intermittent breaks just to drink water as if the water flushes down whatever he is reading and his reaction depicts how essential it is for him to drink the water. He had got over cold but we have really not talked about the experience. Trust me I am going to laugh.

"The cold came like a rush, a kind of wave that I could not fight" Ali explained in a bud to make me understand how he felt when the rush of the cold fell on him. His expression immediately spark up laughter in me but I held on to myself.

"That's quite a crazy feeling, seems like a fever," I said in response.

We both feasted on some snacks late in the afternoon. Sidra was back from where she had gone to plait her hair with the old lady.

"I love the fact that they are both getting along so well," Ali said to me and I nodded in support of his notation.

Their friendship had grown within just a little time, owing to the fact that Sidra is a lovable person, she has this aura within her that always attracts people to her, also she has a good character, pure spirit, and soul. All these are enough reasons to love her.

Now everyone has something to put on to be a guide against the cold because if proper care is not taken, it could result in a severe cough or even chest pain. One must not leave the fire on the mountain unquenched.

CHAPTER NINE

BEEF IN BREAKFAST

Our days in Quetta began to roll by, in due course we were on the hope that we would be here for some days.

Our host had promised to make us breakfast by himself.

"I would love to treat you guys to a delicious breakfast this morning" he proposed to us. This we hopped on without hesitation. The fact that someone wants to make your food without stressing about it goes a long way and also, he is our host, not officially anyway. We must in all ways show appreciation to him for this kind gesture. It is rare in this present day to see someone who will house you and at the same time put food on your table. He definitely should be appreciated.

Sidra offered an assisting hand in the kitchen and in no time, breakfast was ready and even ready to be devoured. Everyone was present at the dining table.

The whole atmosphere is filled with the aroma of the well-sauced stew prepared by our host. We all have been salivating in anticipation of the big dish coming our way pretty soon.

"And this smells like a stew with all the delicious meats in it," Ali said in anticipation of what is coming.

My eyes wandered around, even to the low hibiscus hedge seated outside the window and its many brilliant red bells stood still and intact unruffled. Beyond the edge, the courtyard with its concrete slabs and neatly manicured Bahama grads at the interstices showed no flying dust. Even beyond the courtyard, there is another stretch of the green and red hedge that stood guard against the one-story east wing of the area. Over and beyond the roof, the tops of palm trees at the front swayed with the same lazy ease they display to gentle ocean winds.

Things needed for breakfast were brought in sequential orders. Right from plates to cutlery and pastries. The whole table was set and the big delicacy was set before us all.

I looked at Ali and the expression written all over him says "now let us devour" that is how funny the expression on him reads.

Our host was the one to serve and dish out the food. Everyone took a turn in collecting the dish and from the expression on their faces, one could tell how well the food was with the aroma that filled everywhere.

It was my turn to get my dish but I met a great disappointment along the line. As far as others are going to enjoy this food so well, I am mostly going to miss out on the fun.

I do not blame anyone for that. I am Hindu and by that virtue, I became a vegetarian who in any way does not eat meat or beef. According to our religious virtues and tenets, we are to keep ourselves away from eating meats or beef. By being Hindu, you are automatically a vegetarian. This is a tenet that in no way you must obey and at the same time uphold so as to keep your faith and righteousness.

On the other hand, Ali and Sidra are Muslims who do not have any restrictions against eating beef but are at right to enjoy it.

Our host does not in any way know that I am Hindu. I kept this away from him and his family, it was only my friends that knew I was Hindu

The food brought before us, I could not eat. All because of the vegetarian reality of me being Hindu.

In Hinduism, vegetarianism is the diet of choice. The practice of abstaining from the consumption of meat, be it poultry, seafood, or even flesh of any breed of animal. We believe that this will be in line with nature, compassion, respectful of other forms of life. Although, there are non-vegetarian Hindus they basically eat fish and red meat and not beef, although they eat eggs and other poultry and dairy products. It is believed that doing this reduces pain and suffering for the animals.

"Why don't the Hindus eat meat? I still cannot wrap my head around it" Sidra once asked me about the reason behind Hindus not eating meat or beef.

"It is just our way of life, we do not believe in sacrificing animals" I explained to her.

Our hosts wondered why I could not eat the food and he was prompted to ask why.

"Why are you not eating your meal, don't you like it?" He probed just to know whether I liked the fold or not. Just before I could reply to him, Ali had taken it upon himself to reply to him.

"His doctor had told him not to eat beef a long time ago, due to his health," Ali told him making him feel quite emotional for me.

"Oh, I am so sorry about that" he retorted.

Ali and Sidra had always kept it within them that I am Hindu. If I did not tell you, you would not know about it.

The fact that they are Muslims does not in any way come between our relationship. We maintain a very cordial relationship which has the motto "Religion is not a barrier".

CHAPTER TEN

Journey into the Mountains

Our not long stay here in Quetta would be rid of fun if our quest for exploration was not on the rise or on the increase. The rate at which we adapt to the condition of things in Quetta is as fast as the word fast itself.

Ali has begun to enjoy our stay and Sidra who had long gotten herself acquainted with the situation of things now finds it easier to keep herself together. And here is me, enjoying every day by day bits of our sojourn in a land where we do not know anyone.

Ali's family is still with the thought that he is in Islamabad. I do not have so many issues wherever I am. All that concerns my people is the fact that my wedding ceremony is fast approaching and every minute now seems to count on every dot.

The days are numbered already but our urge to still explore more of Quetta is intact and must be satisfied. The satisfaction derived from this could be second to none as it depicts the natural feel of mother nature and the closeness to the environment.

Quetta is quite blessed with hills and mountains.

"Pretty well hills are around here, would not mind exploring you know?" Ali said inform of a question but we all know better.

"It will really be a great sight to be up there" I submitted as I pointedly describe the height of a mountain opposite. This also shows my positive affirmation of what was said by Ali.

We had earlier been to the nearest amusement park and center, although it was not well planned like we used to while in Islamabad. We had quite a swell experience at the amusement park.

"Let us check out the horses around here" Sidra had forced us out to check out the said horses. The experience down there was worth it and I can literally say we enjoyed every bit of the whole hangout.

Just like we used to do back in Islamabad, we started making arrangements for our trip to the mountains and started putting things in place just to go see some sights. We all were eager and anxious to be atop the mountain.

Ali would as usual be the one in charge of refreshments. Just like a team, we have always had specialized roles dedicated to us based on our strengths and how well we can hold a certain position among us.

The outpour of enthusiasm for this seemed not to thrill our host. He had been looking at us all the while we had been planning. Though he had promised to go with us, he still does not seem enthusiastic as us.

"You do not seem to be excited as we are going to the mountains" I pushed him.

"You guys are just going there for the first time, I have been there countless times, nothing excites me about it anymore," he said in response to my insinuation.

He is definitely right, he was born and brought up here, he grew up with this as a phenomenal part of his environment, hence why he is not as excited as we are, we are only first-timers with a great thirst for exploration.

The early morning dew tried its best at bringing down the day's plan but we found our own way around it. Talk of the monumental display of heavy threat all over the sky and also the weather's threat of a heavy downpour. At first, we had this second thought of going back but Sidra seemed to be extra vigilant and at the same time extra cautious.

After the season of congealed dampness, came to spell a spell of dry frost, when strange birds from behind the North began to arrive silently into the kingdom; gaunt spectral creatures with tragical eyes - eyes which were about to witness scenes of cataclysmal horror in inaccessible polar regions of a magnitude such that no man can ever go through; which had beheld the crash of icebergs and the slide of snow-hills by the shooting light of the aurora; been half-blinded by the whirl of colossal storms and water-filled destruction and retained the expression of the feature that such scene had endangered. These nameless creatures of birds cane quite near to the great mountain but of all the people had seen which humanity would never see, they brought to no account.

We set out a little bit earlier than we used to, with our feet firmly rigid to the ground where our feet are at the same time strong, that nothing would tamper with it.

"The pathway that leads to the mountain is quite stumpy" our host had already told us and I return we are prepared for such obstacles in such a way that we all clad our feet in high-top sneakers.

"I am definitely going to fix myself up," Ali said in support of our actions.

We had to purchase a sweatshirt and cardigan for this. The cold up there could be said to be threefolds of the one being experienced on the lowland.

The journey into the mountains begins and we are all on the lookout for an experience on the mountain which in our mind would not be a disappointment. With the help of our tour guard who in turn is our host, we were able to easily locate the ascending point of the mountain.

"We'll take it up from here," he said as he gives the tour guard instructions and he continues "you have to tread cautiously up here. Seems slippery and sloppy, let us be careful" he sounded the warning into our ears.

We know how well mountains could be slippery during this period, and also the adverse effects of this. We have at the same time prepared for whatever havoc might want to happen and have found solutions to all the seeming loopholes.

"It could be crazy up there, but we are definitely going to love it" our host assured us, this time with much enthusiasm.

As we draw quite closer to the mountain top, the cold hand of the breeze is beginning to get its hands on us despite the fact that we are not even close to the cliff yet. The beautiful overview of the city got so much of our attention and we could see vividly the beautiful city of Quetta. The city is far more beautiful than what we see in the lowlands. Quetta at this point I can sag is such a beautiful city, with the mist that takes over the whole atmosphere.

The mountain top just like others is cold but this particular time of the year, it is colder up here, for the number one raft that we are in Quetta, that is a plus already.

Seeing sights on the mountain personally gives me a kind of inner joy as I could feel a limp within me, that of excitement.

From a very far distance, one could sight the whole of Quetta in a bird's eye view. The tallest building in Quetta seemed to be like a bungalow right from the mountain top, quite an experience.to remember.

We secured a spot atop the mountain for recreational purposes. We had planned earlier before now to stay a little while atop the mountain to at least have a little picnic just the way we used to do in Islamabad.

"We definitely must go with snacks, just the way we have our picnics" Sidra had proposed in the middle of our planning processes. Hangouts and picnics in Islamabad have always been fun with the planning.

As to new things which we just got to discover about Quetta, just up here on the mountain. Right on the mountain also we saw some groups of people who at the same time came to the mountains for recreation also. We exchanged greetings as they moved past us towards where I can call a spot where they would sit.

The time they say there is for everything and one can never predict what would happen. You only need to be calm and see how things unfold with time. The time out on the mountain gives us a fresh opportunity to engage our host, not on an individual or interpersonal level but now as a group. The beauty in this is that we were able to get up and close with our host and vice versa. He opened up on several things which were quite ambiguous to us.

Talks about his daughter, father, and how he ended up being a bus conductor

"I was just some years close to thirty when I gave birth to my daughter, " he said as he gave us a few points about how he came by his five-year-old baby girl. From the way he talks about her, one could see that he is obviously in love with the little girl as he even describes her as his "life".

"I love her so much l, she was given birth to just when my life was taking a turn". One thing I noticed was that he did not say anything about his daughter's mother which prompted none of us to talk about it. I personally thought, maybe it is a part of his own life that he does not love to share or a kind of insecurity he would really not want to let out.

Exciting moments is another name for our hangouts and picnics. The moments we cherish most were the ones we documented. Normally, on picnics, we would take picture photographs and selfie pictures just to mark the moment and make the moment an immortal one.

On the mountain, we snapped pictures of ourselves, selfies, and personal shots which would serve as an archive for the wonderful moments and memories.

Our stories would definitely be rid of references if in any case we were not able to document these moments in pictures and they are quite accessible as we have copies of them on the mobile device that we are with.

"That is one advantage of technology" our host commended.

CHAPTER ELEVEN

MISS YOU

The end has always been the beginning of another journey. Wherever it seems like is an end to something is literally the beginning of another.

Our journey (sojourn) in Quetta was one filled with so many fun and sweet experiences. My friends at the same time enjoyed themselves in such a way that our first experience of a wrong note in Quetta got erased as soon as we saw the beauty of Quetta. We got blown away by all that we saw of the West northern city, the city of excessive cold and mild weather.

"I am overwhelmed at the turn out of things here in Quetta" Ali compliments our stay in Quetta.

Sidra is lowkey happy that she was able to fulfill one of her numerous quests, and at the same time could convince us to find our way to Quetta.

Our Adventures in Quetta would not have been complete without the visit to the mountains. We made sure that every one of our moments on there got documented for future references.

Everything is set for us to move out of Quetta after a quiet experience-filled sojourn in the beautiful land.

"I will miss you all when you are gone, especially Sidra" the sweet old lady had said on one of the

Nights that precede our departure. We are going to miss everyone here equally. It is our wish not to leave but we really have to. We left in Quetta a big family that dwells in love and is ready to share whatever it is with these people. The bonding took quite a short while to achieve but it was totally worth it.

Our stay in Quetta has just come to an end. We need to find our own ways down to the south in order for us to go back to Chelhar, Tharparkar, and at the same time preparing for my wedding ceremony is quite ongoing and a lot of things have to be put in place.

We had intact our luggage and every bit of our things in Quetta even having everything together before our departure. We would not want to lose anything or get to discover that one or more than one of our stuff is missing.

The experience of the lost ring still pounds in my head in such a way that I now get scared whenever I just got something new and I would not want to lose any.

"You are just suffering from PTSD (Physical and Emotional stress), you have to purge this out," Sidra says to me in a quite funny but still serious way. PTSD does not only relate to chronic traumatic experiences but also has to do with the little things to which we tend not to pay quite much attention.

"They come in such a way that you get scared of every little bit of it. It is psychological and most times therapy and counseling sessions are advised" Ali chipped in during one of our conversations.

I never had it in mind to go for any therapy session. These things are just normal things. You would always want to be conscious and extra careful of your previous mistakes, because experience, they say, is the best of teachers. By putting everything into consideration means giving the necessities the needed thoughts and coming to peace with them

We all crept towards a point in the expanse but of shade just at hand which a feeble light was beginning to assert its presence, a spot where, during the day, a fitful white streak of steam at intervals upon the dark green background denoted intermittent moments of contact between our own conscious world and modern life. Modern life stretched out its steam feeler to this point three or four times a day, touched the native existences, and quickly withdrew its feeler again as if what he touched had been uncongenial.

Ali felt he was going to break down a bit after the whole trip but I brought back the confidence in him to look beyond and after all that, we are dealing with at the moment. After this little talk, we decided to take a refreshing walk down the way. We reached the feeble light, which came from the smoky lamp of a little walkway; a poor enough terrestrial star, yet in one sense of more importance to mankind than the celestial ones to which it stood in such humiliating contrast.

We set out to leave Quetta so early in the morning. The initial plan was to move towards the south and journey down to Karachi in such a style that we would have to journey down to my hometown with quite a number of stopovers our way, just to make every part of the journey adventurous.

I have realized the fact that the journey between the north and the down south in Chelhar is almost about 24 hours, hence the reason for the stopovers. The journey would be quite boring and uninteresting if arrangements are not made for the stopovers. At each spot, there are hawkers selling different varieties of edibles that serve as refreshments for tired and weary travelers.

This has saved lots.

"You have to be early to the bus station to secure an early bus to the next destination" Our host had told us earlier the night before, that securing a bus so early would cost us being early to the bus station.

Ali has been the earliest to wake and he has taken the chance to wake us up as early as possible so we can get to hit the road.

"Wake up, it's 8 AM already" Ali raised an alarm in my ears which I reacted to frantically as I sprang up immediately at Ali's alarm. He burst into laughter as soon as he saw my swift reaction.

At the station, we booked our tickets and fortunately for us, our bus moves in thirty minutes. While waiting, we got engulfed in our talks that we almost forgot to buy a little refreshment that would serve as our breakfast but I picked back as early as possible.

"We got something to eat already" my memories sparked back

"No we haven't" Sidra jerked back also. We all scamper towards the women who sell snacks. The women seemed to have been there since last not, some were sleepy while some were extra active.

It's time for passengers to get on board so the journey can start and we get to move.

A sense of excitement descended on us as soon as we bade Quetta goodbye, so early in the cold morning.

We saw ourselves as explorers who had just cleared a cluster web of obstacles in an arduous task to earn as a result the conviction, more by intuition perhaps than logic, that at least the final goal of our adventure still lies hidden beyond more adventures and dangers, the puzzles we just unraveled points crystal clear to imminent and inevitable success.

The journey down towards the south began and we are deep into it. The day is beginning to take form and along the route, we could see people beginning to take to their daily activities. The filled bus drifts round and round whenever it has the chance to and this gives me a type of feeling that is eccentric and out of this world.

Ali is quite enjoying his own company in what we can call a smooth ride. He had been on one of his big books since the beginning of the journey but would look over the window to check whatever was going on outside and at the same time, hoping to get a better sight and view if what so ever, there is anything.

"Are you comfortable that way?" I once asked him, during one of his checks.

"Oh yes, very well" he replied casually and went back to the books he had left.

Sidra on the other hand seems to be juggling different personalities. A part of Ali and quite the reputation of mine. This is anyways not a journey into the badlands.

At the increased speed of the vehicle, I suffered a recurrence of sharp anxiety. But the driver is seen not to be interested in my predicament or ordeal.

The tracks we left behind can only be covered if we come back to Quetta, which is most likely impossible for Ali and me. Karachi is where we would always want to go back to buy Quetta? I am not very sure. But Sidra would want to come back to Quetta. Her friend Sanaya lives here and she always wanted to visit her.

Our fast speeding bus pulled over at a spot for us to stretch our bodies and also for people to ease themselves.

Mostly women and children were the ones who trooped out of the bus to ease themselves while some of the kids ended up playing and at the same time waiting for the driver's order to move. Mostly, drivers on their own do not end up shouting atop their voices for the passengers to enter. I believe everyone is always on the alert for the sound of the bus horn.

At just a honk or two, every passenger would find their way into the bus, if the time elapsed, the bus would move.

Although I have never witnessed where the bus had to leave someone behind because he or she did not make it into the bus on time.

Some drivers are actually merciful enough to look into the vehicle and check if there are vacant seats in the bus which might belong to a passenger who is probably outside or has gone astray.

CHAPTER TWELVE

BUS TO CHELHAR

The thick rain forest of the south which even a great highway snaked like an ordinary game track began to yield ground most grudgingly at first but in time a little more willingly to less prodigious rapid growth coupled with a hundred kilometers further towards the north, but unbelievably to the open parklands of grass and stunted trees. The traveler's spirit and soul rose in step with this diminution of forests which gave the eye a heady facility to roam freely and take in wide panoramas of space stretching to a horizon where tiny trees on distant hills and against clear skies formed miniature gardens.

Even the rate at which buses sped towards the south told quite a story about the two regions. Thickly-laid and cushiony at first it steadily deteriorated into thin black paint applied with niggardly strokes of a feather brush over right beginning to break up and expose, as the journey progressed. More and more of the brown underlay, forcing the elegant and giant bus to lurch from side to side to avoid some deep ruts. But Ali welcomed this disappointment of comfort for the blessing it had in tow, for it curtailed the recklessness of luxurious which had been conducting herself like a termagant of the highway treating her passengers' safety cavalierly and bullying every smaller vehicle encountered clean out of the way as though traffic rights were just a matter of size.

The town and villages on the road responded inappropriate way to the general scaling down in the size of strictures as one pushed out of the rain country slowly towards the land of droughts. The massive buildings of the newly rich people down the coast gave way to less imposing houses and buildings just on the road.

The bus moved towards a path in the expanse but of shade just at hand which a feeble light was beginning to assert its presence, a path where, most of the time during the day, a fitful white streak of steam at intervals upon the dark green surface denoted intermittent moments of contact between the oncoming automobile and natural slippery path, that is rid of smoothness and good frequency. Modern life stretched out its steam feeler to this point three or four times a day, touched the native existences, and quickly withdrew its feeler again as if what he touched had been uncongenial.

Our bus lurched from one side of the road to the other to avoid obstacles that could be dangerous to the bus. Police and army checkpoints at boundaries came and went quite fairly.

The bus had been traveling for quite a little while when it pulled up at a spot for passengers to at least feel the cool breeze. The passengers were glad and excited to escape from the stagnant, cooped-up heat inside the bus into the dry hot waves of the open air. In just a few minutes we are ordered back onto the bus. As the bus plunged deeper into the burning desolation, I reached into my side bag and pulled out a copy of the book Ali had given to me a long while ago. I sunk into this for quite an hour before Ali tapped me and had a swift conversation with me.

"The atmosphere that accompanies this journey seems quite serene and calm," he said and he romanticized the weather and atmosphere. I was sure it was because of the season of the year which gave room for this kind of atmospheric condition.

"The weather is enjoyable "I responded slightly as I tilted my head up from the direction of the book I was reading.

The journey to Karachi in this manner would be a measure to have once again the previous experience.

The initial plan was to be in Karachi for a night and, so we could withdraw our dresses and sherwani from the store where we dropped them earlier for processing. Trip to Karachi once again seems to be like fun even more than the usual fun way that we used to have it.

Normally, traveling with friends is quite expected to be fun and interesting. You get to talk and also rummage and reminisce about several lots, different points of interest also give an edge to the discussion.

The fast speeding bus waves in a way that we could feel how flexible the ride is.

After what seemed like a very long ride, we arrived at the Karachi bus station late in the evening. Just as planned, we are to spend just a night in Karachi with the hope of leaving the city as soon as we recover the dresses from the stores. Sidra had gone immediately to her hostel

Ali and I made our way straight to the hotel where we were lodged earlier and made the reservation for our room. At the reception, we told them about the missing ring.

"We misplaced a new ring the last time we lodged" I lodge my complaint at the reception, making them know and what the ring looks like. The timely intervention of the manager also gave an assurance that if anything comes yo, we would be notified.

We moved as far into the city of Karachi to withdraw all the clothes which we had dropped for processing at different stores. We had earlier selected our choices of designs from various designer brands in and outside Pakistan.

The processing of these wears according to the shops would take quite some days but not as long as we had thought.

"They will take some time in the processing units, although your products are still going to be intact," the store manager told us at the store the previous day we went there.

The shops were known for selling quite original products hence, the reason for the processing and all. This would in a way showcase the standards at which these products are placed in society.

It is in all ways right to even put these stores in consideration when ranking them. With a very high taste, one would likely walk into these stores and see for oneself the height at which these people place luxury. The price on it alone depicts luxury and affluence.

Ali in Karachi had made sure that we did not leave any stone unturned and that he had touched every aspect of the preparation needed in Karachi. To sum everything up, we made sure we bought every other thing needed, even the ones he felt needed but we never mentioned while putting down the list of our wants and needs.

That we are surrounded by deep mysteries is known to all but the incurably ignorant. But even they must concede the fact, indeed the inevitability, of the judiciously spaced, but certain, interruptions in the flow of their high art to interject the word of their sponsor, the divinity that controls the remote but diligently the transactions of the marketplace that is their world.

Ali has been a good assistant all along in this process and it is fair enough to say he has tried. Right from our journey from Islamabad to Karachi, he had been my watchman making sure everything was intact and at the same time in the position, they are supposed to be.

He knows fully well everything that comes with all we are doing and at most our journey ends in my hometown and the utmost goal here is to make sure my wedding ceremony is a success. Meanwhile, bringing my friends along with me is not only for my friends but at the same time for myself. Me bringing people of this such status is quite honorable of me and it speaks a whole bunch about who I am in society.

The implication of what we do today is what tomorrow resonates. If we could give today a better definition and reshape its structure, we'll be setting a pace on which tomorrow would stand.

After getting the whole process done, a call was placed through to Sidra, who had been relaxing at her hotel, just to make know that we are set and ready to move out of Karachi already. Although, earlier in the morning, we had called and informed her about our plan to leave that afternoon.

"We would be leaving Karachi in a couple of moments," I said to her over the phone.

"I wish you a safe trip brothers, see you guys soon" she also bade her farewell.

We moved from the hotel straight to the bus station. There we got quite lucky enough, the passengers on the ground were not as many as they would be on a usual weekday. We made payments for our tickets in no time and were waiting for the takeoff time.

"Passengers should be ready and be on the alert" a loud voice instructs over the microphone and then continues "Buses move in the next thirty minutes" On hearing this, passengers started moving their luggage and also they started moving towards the bus. Ali and I were already on the alert for this, waiting for the take-off time. We got our place on the bus and were ready to journey to my hometown.

Our trip to Chelhar is one of a kind. We had one of my smoothest journeys so far. Right from the bus station in Karachi, the bus was as comfortable as possible, with each passenger to their own space in the bus. No wonder people tag such vehicles as "AC Bus". The comfort that comes with this bus is top-class and an executive tier. The stopovers on the roads were quite a few as the distance from our point of departure to the destination is not so far, hence stopovers were unnecessary.

The distinction of this vehicle, though by no means a subtle one, was yet too subtle for the route it is plying. It went on the road as fly as it could. The driver would also accelerate in a manner that makes the subtlety and swiftness of the ride mire fascinated. I was glad I was on the bus. The journey to Chelhar would have been as stressful as hell if it were not for the efficiency and comfortability of the said AC bus.

The journey seemed to be faster than usual and in a few hours, we touched down at the Bus station in Mithi where we would take another bus to the not-so-far Chelhar.

On the bus to Chelhar, Ali and I slept so well but never forgot where we were to alight.

The excitement on them when we got home was out of this world. The happiness radiating all over their faces is ethereal.

And now the time has come for me to see my people again after years of being away from them. Today no one can rise and march by starlight abandoning crippled kindred in the wild savannah and arrive stealthily in a small village and fall upon its inhabitants. No one precisely exists in a vacuum; we all are deeply rooted in one set of people or the other. Here, the people are excited to have me around.

"Now you have grown up to become a really big man," one of the elders said as he patted me on the back. Even without saying it, one could read that this has been on their mind because you can deduce such from their facial expressions. The fact is that they would be wondering how the boy of yesterday had grown so old to become. The feeling of being treated like a celebrity in your own country home is a way to show how well you have represented the community so well. Such an ambassador is what I am.

" I am so happy and proud of what you have turned out to become," my mother said in my praise. Seeing me after this many years gives her a joy she cannot explain herself. The smile that lit up our faces was quite indefatigable. It was just like a moment of reunion, just like the ending of an exile. The return of a union that both parties have severely missed.

The love I have for my mother is out of this world and anything I do or become on this day will always be dedicated to her for her love and care for me.

Her only son had gone for so many years and now he is back, being celebrated by all and sundry.

The sense of excitement that had descended on me the whole time stayed with me all day, and I could say I loved the way I felt. For quite some time, I had assumed quite naively that happiness depends solely on the self and if you're not happy with yourself, then Spreading happiness would be quite hard.

My family had taken a turn at meeting Ali. Right from our arrival, my father and brother met Ali and they all got along quite well together. They expressed their gladness towards Ali's presence at the wedding and also appreciate him for his kind gestures.

"I appreciate you. You have been a very good friend to my son. He has said a lot about you, and we can see you are just as how he described you" my father had said, Ali.

My uncles also came around to meet with Ali and also have some words with him.

They presented some ornaments to Ali just in appreciation of what he had done and also his commitment to the success of the wedding

My family made a large banquet of dinner to celebrate my arrival. Ali especially was the distinguished guest of the night; he was superbly treated just like the king that he is. One could see the undaunted love showered on my friend which portrays the pure union that exists between us all.

The dinner avails my family members the opportunity to get more familiar with Ali. It developed later into a mind of meet and greet as everyone wants to ask him one thing or the other.

By this time, it was getting late at night. Ali is to be in the guest room. My Brother had made arrangements for the room especially for Ali who they treated like a special guest.

I spent the night with Ali in the guest room just to keep his company and not make the night get boring for him. We had some words over the night which made us go over our experiences in the past few years, especially our moments at University in Islamabad.

The journey down towards the south could be quite stressful as anyone would know. The night is beginning to fall heavy and to take form and activities all around the area had calmed so well by mow The whole house seems like a deserted one because of the deep silence that has quietly dwelled on the house, everyone has retired to bed, even the kids that have been running all around had slept like logs of wood.

Ali is quite enjoying our own company in what we can call smooth talk. He had both been none or two topics since we retired into the beds. Ali on his end is enjoying the company and the smoothness of our conversation. There are bits of lessons in them and precisely some things or chapters that we have never opened.

It was getting late into the middle of the night, and I observed that Ali might not just be so comfortable with the way he is on the bed.

"Are you comfortable that way?" I once asked him, as soon as I noticed the posture.

"Oh yes, very well" he replied me casually, and I could see that he was slippering into slumber.

My mind wanders to Sidra in Karachi. I thought about how we had all met in Islamabad and the kind of relationship we have maintained since then till the present day. If not for her, we would not have gone to Quetta which is in no way regret.

CHAPTER THIRTEEN

OVER

The night here set so early and people we just as ready to go to bed and hit the hay. Ali and I were still up, although tired but still wanted to catch up with so many things, the talks about our sojourn in Islamabad and also the turn that our studies took. Although never a bad turn, we on our own turned out so well, so no point to regret it.

Almost at midnight, we received a call from the hotel where we were lodged in Karachi, reporting to us that your missing ring had been found and they had made preparations for its pickup.

"We found a ring right on the wardrobe in the room where you were lodged in our facility" the masculine voice had said over the phone, still affirming that they had found my missing ring already. That alone beamed some light of hope.

"Oh wow, that is incredibly great" I retorted in surprise as I could not even hide how happy I am.

We had before leaving Karachi told the hotel authority about the missing ring but we never knew they would find it or even would be found in the hotel.

Ali would be going to Karachi from Chelhar. My friend Sunil Tharani would be the one to take Ali over to the

Bus Station where he would board a bus to Karachi. The distance between Karachi and Chelhar is not as far as it would only take up a few hours and it is only just four days to my wedding ceremony.

At exactly 3:00 AM, I put a call to my good friend Sunil Tharani, whom I informed about the change in plans and at the same time, had to request his help.

"Dheeraj, this is so early in the morning, I hope there is no problem" Sunil speaks over the phone with his croaky voice that has embedded in it some more elements of sleep and slumber.

"It is no problem, we are in Chelhar already but my friend needs to leave for Karachi as early as 4 AM. I need you to help take him to the Mithi bus station where he would secure a ride to Karachi" I pleaded with Sunil who accepted immediately.

"This is 3 AM, let us meet at the square by 4 AM and I would take him to the bus station", he said assuring me of his support and help.

Swiftly, Ali and I made quite well preparations for the trip. Ali tidied up everything and as it was 4 AM he was ready to take off. I called Sunil to also notify him and to my utmost surprise, he was ready and also ready to move.

"I am only waiting on you so you know what next step to take," he says over the phone when I pulled a call through

We moved to the square where Sunil would be taking Ali to the Mithi bus station so he could be on his way down to Karachi. Another journey ahead.

"I will take him to Mithi, there he would get a bus to Karachi," Sunil said as they were about to leave.

They departed just to embark on the 350KM journey from Mithi to Karachi. Ali definitely would enjoy the journey down there and also the adventures and fun he would derive from his visit back to the hotel and also to the market where he would get to buy a list of new things which just hot included in my list.

As soon as Ali got to Karachi in the noon, he wasted no time as he took to straight to the hotel to receive the ring from the hotel manager who had called earlier to inform us about the found ring.

"Thank goodness, exactly ours" Ali had told me over the phone. I heaved a sigh of relief as soon as I heard this. Asides from the money used in purchasing this ring, its beauty stands it out and it is exactly why I fell in love with it.

He definitely would want to do some other things and flex his muscles a little bit.

He knows fully well everything that comes with all we are doing and at most our journey ends in my hometown and the utmost goal here is to make sure my wedding ceremony is a success. Meanwhile, bringing my friends along with me is not only for my friends but at the same time for myself. Me bringing people of this such status is quite honorable of me and it speaks a whole bunch about who I am in society.

I on the other hand back home has a lot on my neck to make come through, right from the need to attend to a teeming crowd of good wishers who had come all out to celebrate with our family to the unending want and demand of people because we need to procure some things and money is essential in doing this.

The sense of excitement that had descended on me the whole time stayed with me all day, and I could say I loved the way I felt. For quite some time, I had assumed quite naively that happiness depends solely on the self and if you're are not happy with yourself, then Spreading happiness would be quite hard.

My mother had invited a handful of friends. The inspiration behind this is what I could not fathom because my mother is not like that. The intention was a traditional wedding. At an earlier time, she would not have had it done that way and, she was normally completely retreated to herself but the years that rolled by have sprung everything loose and up by personality and the kind of environment she lives in.

But maybe she could return less and less timidly to the relive aspect of her own life and even begin to reassess her reflexes, feelings, and at the same time thoughts.

Ali had earlier promised to come to Chelhar with Sidra. After collecting the ring from the hotel, he had placed a call through to her to inform her about their journey to Chelhar which she also made no fuss about. The duo departed Karachi quite earlier than I thought and I believe they got a bus quite right on time.

They landed in Chelhar safe and sound with the bulk of the goods they had brought with them.

My sisters fell in love with Sidra, on a normal basis, who would not.

Now the hustle and bustle is over, let the ceremony begin.

Quetta

Dheeraj Kumar was born and brought up in the Desert Tharparkar, Pakistan. He is a Freelancer, author, blogger, and Photographer. Dheeraj did his Bachelor's degree in Software Engineering and now works at a software firm as a Web Developer and Technical Writer. He resides with his family in Tharparkar.
"Every man holds inspiration, You have to have a seeing Eye". - Dheeraj Kumar

www.ingramcontent.com/pod-product-compliance
Lightning Source LLC
Chambersburg PA
CBHW022027150726

47990CB00002B/844